The Transatlantic Slave Trade

A Captivating Guide to the Atlantic Slave Trade and Stories of the Slaves That Were Brought to the Americas

Free Bonus from Captivating History
(Available for a Limited time)

Hi History Lovers!

Now you have a chance to join our exclusive history list so you can get your first history ebook for free as well as discounts and a potential to get more history books for free! Simply visit the link below to join.

Captivatinghistory.com/ebook

Also, make sure to follow us on Facebook, Twitter and Youtube by searching for Captivating History.

Contents

Introduction

History is often filled with mesmerizing stories, great feats, and accomplishments. It fills us with pride to learn about our past and ancestors. As such, we tend to gravitate toward tales of great heroes, wise men and women, and geniuses. It's always about the achievements our predecessors attained and the hurdles they overcame. Those parts of our history are often comforting and give us all a feeling of hope for our own future. However, we should also remember the dark side of our past, even if it's less comfortable for us to confront it. Especially if those bygone days of our shared story of humanity still casts a shadow on our present times.

One such gloomy aspect of our history is the story of the Atlantic slave trade. It is part of our past that is often skipped or merely touched upon in our schools, conveniently left on the sidelines of our historical consciousness. In all aspects, this is a story of how inhumane humans can be to each other, especially when it comes down to material gain and profit. As such, it exhibits some of the vilest sides of our nature, making it quite appealing for the public to just acknowledge it existed without delving any deeper into how the slave trade began, grew, and evolved before it was finally stopped. This guide is an attempt to explore this shameful part of our past without any beautification and justification.

However, this doesn't mean this book would just condemn the atrocities and move on. We will explore how they came about, under what circumstances, and how it evolved over time. Parts of these stories may become a bit gritty, yet it is important to face those head on to fully grasp the severity of slavery. Nonetheless, the macabre isn't the purpose of this book. Our goal is to get a broad perspective on the issue. A large chunk of our history, roughly from the late 14th to the early 19th century, will be covered, while our geographical scope will touch on both shores of the Atlantic Ocean. We will examine the involvement of several major nations in this despicable trade, from the Portuguese to the Americans, while also shedding light on the involvement of the Africans themselves. However, slave traders and owners won't be the only topic of this guide. We'll depict the lives and treatment of the ones unfortunate enough to be captured and exported, giving an insight into their misery and condition.

As such, with this broad approach, there will be some generalizations and simplification, yet hopefully, it will be enough for you to get a basic picture of this historical development. Our aim with this guide is to leave you sufficiently informed as well as intrigued enough for you to dive deeper into this complicated and rather important topic, whose echoes still shape our world today.

Chapter 1 – Slavery through the Ages and across Continents

As with many historical themes, slavery is generally often oversimplified and misrepresented, dotted with misconceptions and half-truths. For many, it is represented by an image of a person hauling rock or gathering cotton under the sound of a whip. However, that is just the tip of the iceberg, as this issue runs much deeper. Because of that, before tackling the specifics of the Atlantic slave trade, it is important to understand slavery in its more universal form.

The roots of slavery run deep, as it is present throughout the written history of humanity. Evidence for it can be found in Egyptian wall paintings, the Babylonian code of Hammurabi (the oldest code of law from the 18th century BCE), or even the Bible. However, historians tend to think the practice of slavery predates the ancient civilizations. Though it is impossible to pinpoint when the first slave was captured, it is presumed this didn't happen before the Neolithic Agricultural Revolution. This momentous transformation happened around 10,000 years ago, as humans began their conversion from hunter-gatherer to sedentary agricultural societies. This would have allowed for a necessary food surplus for maintaining a slave workforce. Nonetheless, some scholars point out that some later hunter-gatherer societies, like the atypical resource-abundant Pacific Northwest Native American tribes, also held slaves. Thus, it is possible that slavery is even older than agriculture. Regardless, this practice certainly became more widespread as early civilizations developed.

These early slaves were most likely prisoners of war, who were captured and then minimally fed to labor for their masters. They had no rights and were treated similarly to other domesticated animals like mules or cattle. This is the basic form of slavery, known as chattel slavery, where persons were denied their humanity and treated as mere property. As such, their masters had the right to do with them as they pleased. Slaves were usually forced to work harsh jobs whenever and wherever their owners ordered them. Besides hard labor, women were sometimes used for pleasure. As property, they were also sold and bought, inherited, or even given away as presents. Slave owners also had a right to punish their slaves in any way and form, including murder. These harsh measures weren't necessarily tied to punishment, as, like with any piece of property, their owners could actually harm them for amusement or for whatever other reason one could engage in such inhumane behavior. However, these outbursts were rare, as slaves were usually seen as valued possessions; thus, unnecessary harm was avoided as much as possible. Overall, when it comes to chattel slavery, masters had the utmost control over the lives of their slaves, basically eliminating the basic principle of free will.

This type of slavery proved to be the most widespread throughout history, as almost all societies around the globe have used it at some point. However, there were some variations to how the enslaved people were seen and handled by societies. For example, in some societies, like in ancient Egypt, slaves could marry among themselves but also with free people. Yet, in others, like among the Romans, these marriages were illegal. Furthermore, in ancient China, two married slaves couldn't be separated, though their children could be taken from them and sold. In contrast, Babylonian or Siamese slave families were legal, but they could have been broken apart by their master's will.

Similar differences could be traced to the right of property. For example, in the Islamic world, Muscovy, and ancient India, slaves couldn't own anything; anything they owned would automatically belong to their owners. In contrast, in Assyria and medieval Mongolia, enslaved people were given the right of property. The Romans stood on the middle ground on this issue, as Roman slaves could technically manage, accumulate, and own property, though their owners could take it away from them at any time. It gave the enslaved an incentive to work harder, hoping that they would gather enough wealth to buy their freedom while their masters still retained overall control.

Roman mosaic depicting slaves serving their masters. Source: https://commons.wikimedia.org

Other examples of how the enslaved have been viewed throughout history and across various cultures can be seen in the various laws regarding slaves. In some societies, like in ancient Rome and the later medieval Byzantine Empire, killing a slave, especially one not belonging to the murderer, was relatively equated with murdering a free person. In the Islamic world and ancient Mesopotamia, killing a slave was seen as merely destroying one's property, and the perpetrator simply had to "repay the damages." In that aspect, the dehumanization of the enslaved was pushed to the extreme. By denying them their humanity, they were seen as subhuman, on a level of a domesticated animal, or as the simple possession of their owner.

Another important difference was society's approach to the sexual abuse of enslaved people, mostly regarding women. It was commonly believed that slaves belonged both in body and soul to their owner. Thus, many societies, like, for example, ancient Athens and various African and Middle Eastern cultures, accepted that masters had the right to demand sexual satisfaction with their slaves. In other places, some restrictions were made. The Chinese and Lombard laws prohibited the rape of married enslaved women, while in medieval Russia, sexual abuse of female slaves was fully banned. This range of approaches to sexual abuse was much narrower when it came to women abusing their male slaves. In most cases, the slave was seen as the offender and was often put to death. Examples of this can be found in ancient Rome and Greece. However, in some cases, like in medieval Byzantium, both the female owner and the abused slave were executed.

There were many other differences in approaches to slavery and enslaved people, but there are just too many to list them all. That fact alone helps to paint the picture of just how widespread servitude was, both through history and in geography. However, the mentioned differences were mostly based on laws or some kind of written records. In that aspect, it is important to note that having legal rights or protection of some sort on paper didn't necessarily equate to reality. As such, it is possible that laws weren't fully enforced or were outright ignored, making the lives of the enslaved even worse than legal theory would let us believe.

Regardless, slavery never became a truly humane act, nor did anyone actually wish to be in such a position. Yet, as civilizations and organized states grew, so did the number of enslaved people. This increase can be accounted for by several major factors. One is rather simple—better-organized states could muster larger armies, which, in turn, led to more people being captured in wars. As was stated before, a large portion of slaves were prisoners of war. The second explanation is that in most societies, children who were born to slaves were also seen as the property of their masters. This meant that over the generations, the slave population would at least partially regenerate or even multiply if the living conditions weren't too rough. Some notable exceptions from this were the Mesoamerican Aztecs, who believed that children shouldn't suffer because of their parents.

Slavery also expanded because bonded labor became an accepted form of servitude. This is also known as debt slavery, and it arose in antiquity as a way to repay one's loans. As with chattel slavery, this form of servitude was quite varied. Sometimes it was voluntary, and sometimes it was forced. In some cases, the family heads would "pawn" their family members to repay their debts. However, there is a striking difference between debt and chattel slavery, as a bonded laborer, at least in theory, would be set free once the loan was paid off. Furthermore, in debt slavery, an enslaved person usually was a member of the same social group as their master. This meant that the maltreatment of indebted slaves was less socially accepted, especially as it was expected that, at some point, they would regain their freedom and become fully functional members of the same social class. Additionally, sharing the same background sometimes prompted more compassion from the owners, unlike captured foreigners in chattel slavery.

Another reason for the growth of slavery in antiquity was the rise of the slave trade. As the economic gain of owning enslaved labor became more apparent, it prompted some people to begin trading in slaves, as they were seen as a commodity like any other. Economically speaking, this created the demand for more enslaved people, as wealthy people would have an interest in buying more slaves while not actively participating in wars to capture their own. In turn, some people turned to catching and enslaving people, creating a new source of supply. However, slave traders didn't necessarily capture people on their own. They usually bought and then resold enslaved people from other sources, sometimes transporting them across significant distances to other slave markets. Overall, slavery was becoming a business like any other.

With the growth of slavery, a differentiation between the nations began to arise in terms of how widespread it was. For example, ancient China and Egypt practiced slavery very early on, yet the overall percentage of their enslaved population was low. Some estimates put the slave population in Shang China (2nd millennium BCE) at about 5 percent. It is likely it grew under later dynasties, yet it seems it never constituted a more substantial part of the population. Similar numbers could also be assumed for the Egyptians. However, both these civilizations are known to have used corvée labor systems as part of taxation. Some argue this forced labor is also a form of slavery, though not all scholars agree with such sentiments, as people retained their freedom and served only a couple of days a year, mostly on public projects.

In contrast, other nations continued to amass more and more enslaved people, transforming from so-called slave-owning societies, which had a low percentage of slaves compared to the total population, into full-on slave societies, where they made up a more considerable proportion. One of the earliest examples of such a development was ancient Athens, where despite the ideals of freedom and democracy, roughly 30 percent of the population was enslaved, according to modern estimates. A similar percentage is linked with the Roman Empire, at least on the Italian Peninsula. In these societies, it is clear much of the work was burdened on the enslaved, who constituted large portions of the population. Another similar development was seen in the Islamic world, for example, in the Abbasid Caliphate (8th–13th century CE). Abbasid rulers and elites continued to import slaves both to serve as workers and as soldiers. In some regions, like in sugar-rich southern Iraq, a local slave population could go up to 50 percent. Yet overall, the slaves constituted a much smaller percentage, probably more similar to the Greeks or Romans.

Islamic slave trade in 13th-century Yemen. Source: https://commons.wikimedia.org

It is worth noting that the Islamized states in Africa also adopted the practice of slavery, quickly rising to the levels of slave societies. The medieval states of Ghana (4th-12th century) and Mali (13th- 16th century), for example, had an enslaved population that counted roughly 30 percent. Other African nations also had high numbers of slaves. Thus, slavery predated the Atlantic slave trade, though in some cases, the percentages of the enslaved population grew in later centuries. During the medieval period, Europe saw a decrease in slavery as it transformed into a Christian civilization. Yet the idea of slavery was far from gone. For example, in the English Domesday Book (1086), roughly 10 percent of the population was marked as slaves. Thus, despite being somewhat frowned upon by some religious leaders, slavery persisted in Europe throughout medieval times.

However, due to the decline of slavery during this period, Europe turned toward serfdom. Serfs were in a somewhat better position than actual slaves, yet their position was somewhat similar. For example, their freedom of movement was limited, usually to the village and its surrounding. They could travel farther only with consent from their feudal lords. However, their personal connection wasn't as much with their overseer than with the land. As such, they actually accompanied sales and purchases of the land; they weren't personally sold as individuals. Because of that, they had much more liberties than slaves, especially in the way they spent their lives; they just had to make sure they paid their tributes and labor taxes. However, in some cases, their lords could meddle in their private lives. For example, in some regions, feudal masters needed to approve marriages or had the right to force their subordinates into their religion. Of course, it is important to note that this kind of relationship wasn't at all unique to Europe, as it was also widely used across the world, from China and Japan to the Islamic world. Additionally, it is vital to mention that serfdom usually coexisted with slavery as well.

As the medieval period entered its later stages, the Christian Church began to openly voice its opposition toward slavery, at least when it came to Christians owning Christians. Even worse was the idea of selling fellow Christians to the "infidels," in this case meaning the Muslims, who had the largest slave market in the late medieval period. As such, these forms of slavery were prohibited by the pope on several occasions. However, such compassion toward human lives was limited only to Christians, as by the 15th century, religious leaders gave open permission for European leaders to enslave Muslims, pagans, and anyone else who were infidels in the eyes of the Church. With such a moral carte blanche, Europeans entered the age of exploration and colonization. It wasn't long before they began exercising their "rights," enslaving large numbers of Africans, who they transported mainly to the Americas but also to Europe. The transatlantic slave trade was born.

Before delving into more details about how this came to be and how this trade of human beings developed through the centuries, it is vital to briefly classify the form of slavery in the new European colonies. Most, if not all, of the Africans were chattel slaves, with virtually no rights at all. Their lives were fully in the hands of their European masters, who usually held them in little regard. Thanks to racism, the Europeans saw colored slaves as lesser beings than them. This idea of Africans being less human was only widened by a civilizational superiority complex, which many of the colonizers had rooted in them. As such, most Europeans saw the slaves merely as work animals, while religious beliefs often washed away any residual feelings of moral guilt.

Additionally, the colonies in the Americas quickly turned from slave-owning to full-on slave societies. The enslaved population grew quickly, in some places becoming the undisputed majority over the whites and what was left of the indigenous population. Thanks to both the large numbers of slaves and the harsh treatment they endured, slavery became one of the most vital and recognizable parts of American colonial history, leaving deep traces in societies on both sides of the Atlantic. It is exactly because of this that we must learn about our past, even if it serves as a reminder of how atrocious humans can be to each other.

Chapter 2 – The Transatlantic Pioneers: The Roles of Portugal and Spain

When talking about the Atlantic slave trade, people tend to focus on the later periods when the British and French dominated the market of forced human labor. However, the roots of this issue began in the early days of European exploration, predating the so-called discovery of the Americas. The Portuguese, the first Europeans since the ancient times to explore the African coast and the Atlantic Ocean, were the ones who started it.

The story of the transatlantic slave trade begins in the early 15th century with the Age of Discovery, when the Europeans realized there was more of the world than their own continent. The impetus for this was partially made by the Ottoman conquests in the eastern Mediterranean, as they slowly but consistently replaced the Byzantines as the linchpin in trade between East Asia and Europe. This was an important event, as the Ottoman Turks began to impede the trade with Christian Europe, limiting the import of highly sought spices and sugar to the high-class Europeans who had become increasingly interested in their use. Other events, like the fall of the Mongol

Empire in Central Asia, further diminished the scope of trade between Asia and Europe. This slowly increased the cost and value of said spices, finally giving an incentive to medieval traders to find other routes to Asia, hoping to reap fiscal gain by bypassing the Turks.

Simultaneously, in the southwestern tip of Europe, on the Iberian Peninsula, Portugal and the Spanish states were engaged in the so-called Reconquista. They fought wars against Muslim states that occupied the southern parts of the peninsula. During those wars, the Christian kingdoms were given a papal decree that permitted the enslavement of non-Christians. Slowly, a slave population, mainly consisting of Moors and Berbers, began to grow as slavery became more common in the region. However, the Muslim states stretched farther south, across northern Africa, prompting further interest in the exploration of the continent. The Portuguese, in particular, wanted to find out how far the power of their Muslim enemies stretched. An even more interesting question was if they could profit from it, either by conquest or by plunder. Thus, the Portuguese, whose Reconquista ended roughly around 1415, began exploring the African Atlantic coast. At first, their focus was on the Moroccan coast, yet in the following years, the Portuguese expeditions traveled farther south, reaching the Senegal and Gambia Rivers.

These explorations were led by the famous Prince Henry the Navigator. The initial goals of his expeditions had nothing to do with slaves but rather the hunger for gold, spices, and conflict with Muslims. However, by the early 1440s, the first slaves were brought by the Portuguese to Europe. According to sources, there were 235 prisoners of war, and one-fifth of them was presented to the royal family of Portugal. By 1444, Henry the Navigator began selling enslaved people from sub-Saharan Africa. However, it wasn't long before the Portuguese abandoned slave-hunting raids, as they proved to be too costly and inefficient. Instead, around 1448, they switched to trade instead, mimicking the already existing slave market. With that, the Portuguese simply tapped into the already existing trade network that had been created long before by the Muslim and local African merchants. Even then, the slaves were far from being the primary "commodity" of the Portuguese traders. Their main goal was gold, for which they often traded back their slaves.

Portrait of Henry the Navigator (top) and illustration of Portuguese navy (bottom). Source: https://commons.wikimedia.org

The number of enslaved people transported back to Europe was relatively small. It is estimated that the Portuguese annually brought about 1,000 enslaved people to Europe after 1448, rising to roughly 2,000 by the end of the century. It constituted about one-third of the total humans traded by the European merchants. In contrast, around two-thirds of enslaved people were traded back to the Africans for gold. Yet the limited scope and the end destination weren't the only differentiators between these early Atlantic slaves and those who lost their freedom just a couple of decades later. Most, if not all, of those initial chattel persons were destined to work as household servants, not as laborers in the fields or mines. This meant that, in part, their lives were somewhat easier overall. However, that was quick to change.

By the time of Prince Henry's death in 1460, Portugal had established its first footholds of their future colonial empire. Its first trading posts were established on the Atlantic islands of Madeira, Cape Verde, the Azores, and Arguin. Afterward, the Portuguese continued their exploration farther south, reaching the Congo River and establishing ports in São Tomé, an island in the Gulf of Guinea, and Elmina on the African coast in what is today Ghana. After these major steps in the 1470s and 1480s, Portuguese sailors reached the southern tip of Africa in 1488 and went on to explore and discover east Africa and India. By that time, Spain also entered the race, taking firm hold of the Canary Islands in the late 15th century. In 1492, the Spanish finally "rediscovered" America after the voyage of Christopher Columbus, who sought to find an alternate route to India and bypass the Portuguese naval monopoly over the African coast. By the 1500s, Portugal established itself in modern-day Brazil, while the Spaniards established their first colonies on the island of Hispaniola in the Caribbean.

As the explorers discovered new naval routes and lands previously unknown to the Europeans, a major shift began on the other side of the Atlantic. While the two Iberian states settled islands off the coast of Africa, they realized they were not only suitable for establishing harbors and trading settlements, but they also had the potential for agriculture. Some, like the Canary Islands, had some local population, while others, like São Tomé, was uninhabited. Nonetheless, both Portugal and Spain began importing African slaves to boost their workforce, especially on the highly valuable sugar plantations. Thus, the Atlantic slave trade began its transformation. However, it was a slow process and rather low in raw numbers. The plantations were small and needed only a limited labor force. Furthermore, in the case of the Canaries, the Spaniards initially tried enslaving the local population. Yet this population quickly stopped being a substantial source of human labor. It was initially small, and it was cut down by European diseases and harsh working conditions. Those who escaped captivity quickly merged with the Spanish colonizers. Because of that, they were quickly replaced by the Africans, who mostly came from sub-Sahara and Morocco.

The story of the Canary Islands was to become a small-scale example of what was going to happen in the Americas. But thanks to its small population and closeness to the Iberian Peninsula, its destiny quickly turned in another direction. Soon, Spanish settlers came and became a significant unchained labor force, further cutting down on the influx of slaves. A similar thing happened on other Atlantic islands under Portuguese rule. As such, these islands saw only a limited number of enslaved when it came to trade. For example, it is estimated that the Portuguese slave merchants traded about 81,000 people, out of whom roughly 60,000 went to Europe. About 3,500 were sent to São Tomé, while another 17,500 were shipped to the Atlantic islands, like Madeira and the Azores. Yet the winds of change began. Not only did the overall volume of slaves grow, but so did the distance between destinations.

The end of the 15th century also brought another important development. Spain and Portugal signed a treaty in 1494, dividing the sphere of their influence and rights in the discovered and yet undiscovered lands. The Treaty of Tordesillas, as it became known, gave the Portuguese rights on the African coast as well as on any land up to 370 leagues west of the Cape Verde Islands. That land was dubbed Brazil, and the Portuguese began settling it around 1516. Yet, more importantly for the transatlantic slave trade, it meant that the slave trade was legally in the hands of the Portuguese merchants, as the Spaniards weren't allowed to sail to Africa and acquire slaves on their own. It's worth noting that other nations gave little regard to the treaty, most notably other future colonial powers, such as the Dutch, the British, and the French, but their presence in the early 16th century was limited by their own weaknesses. Regardless, it proved vital for the shaping of the transatlantic slave trade's future.

This allowed the Portuguese to focus on entrenching their control over the African coast. For the most part, it was peaceful, with the Portuguese gaining trade agreements with the local kingdoms, most notably the Kingdom of Kongo in western-central Africa. It allowed the Portuguese to buy Kongolese prisoners of war, as well as any other captives. Their presence in this part of the African continent was only furthered in the 1570s when the Kongo allowed and even encouraged the Portuguese to take control of what is today Angola. In 1575, the city and port of Luanda was formed, becoming yet another important point of the Portuguese slave trade network. With that, the area of modern-day Congo and Angola became one of the primary sources of enslaved people, surpassing the initial Senegambian, Gold Coast, and Gulf of Guinea regions. By modern estimates, western-central Africa accounted for almost 40 percent of enslaved people shipped across the Atlantic Ocean.

At the same time, the Canary Islands and São Tomé were further developed, as they were sugar-producing regions, with slave labor as its main driving force. By the mid-16th century, other Atlantic islands lagged behind them in that aspect. Those two became the forerunners in sugar production, both due to their climates and suitable fertility but also since it was rather close to the source of the enslaved people. However, as the Europeans discovered more of the Americas and as they conquered more of its lands, a new market for the slave workforce opened up. By the early 1500s, the first slaves were transported to the Spanish holdings in the Caribbean, essentially transforming the Atlantic slave trade into the transatlantic slave trade. Nonetheless, in the early years, the number of enslaved people transported across the Atlantic Ocean was rather small, as were the colonial possessions. Unfortunately, that number would rise quickly in the second half of the 16th century.

According to a conservative estimate from modern scholars, by the end of the century, the Portuguese trafficked slightly more than 240,000 African slaves. A small percentage, just below 25,000, went to Europe, and about 18,000 were shipped to the Atlantic islands. São Tomé became the epicenter of the slave trade, with approximately 75,000 unfortunate souls ending their journey there. Due to its geographical location, São Tomé also became a springboard for transporting enslaved people across the Atlantic to the new colonies. In contrast, the entire Spanish colonial empire in the Americas, including modern-day Mexico, Jamaica, Cuba, and many other islands, imported roughly the same number of slaves as São Tomé. In the latter half of the century, Brazil became an avid importer of forced labor, reaching around 50,000 imported slaves. It is also important to keep in mind that these estimates are on the lower end, as some scholars think they may be four times larger, totaling nearly one million souls by 1600. Regardless, the numbers are immense, considering that, for example, the Portuguese capital of Lisbon boasted a population of 150,000 in 1600, while London reached about 200,000 at the same time. Thus, even the lowest estimates are larger than the total population of some of Europe's largest cities.

Portuguese explorations and colonies. Source: https://commons.wikimedia.org

The numbers paint a picture of how extensive human trafficking was, but they don't answer the question of why it expanded to such an extent in the Americas. A somewhat simplified answer is a labor shortage. When the Spaniards and the Portuguese began establishing proper colonies in their American domains, they initially turned to sugar as their source of income. Both the Caribbean islands and Brazil had fertile lands and a suitable climate for growing such a valuable commodity. It was seen as the best way to repay the costs of long voyages and expensive conquests. However, sugar production was labor intensive, and the colonists lacked the workforce to farm it efficiently. Not to mention many of them went to the Americas to get rich without having to work hard. Initially, both the Spanish and the Portuguese turned toward an existing labor pool, that of the Amerindians. There were an estimated twenty-five million natives in Mexico alone, with many more in other regions. However, the native population suffered a demographic collapse during the 16th century due to their struggles against the Europeans, which included the social disruption caused by the conquerors and, most notably, the numerous illnesses the Europeans brought with them.

Furthermore, the hard labor on the sugar plantations proved to be too much of a strain on the locals, who were less physically capable than the Africans. On top of that, many of the natives, especially from the regions that lacked highly developed civilization, like, for example, the Brazilian coast, rarely practiced large-scale agriculture. That made the natives look less effective in the eyes of their colonial masters. An additional problem in certain regions was that the Amerindians lacked knowledge in ironworking, unlike the Africans, who were acquainted with metallurgy. The local native population also proved more troublesome to control. Since they were captives on their own land with clearly defined oppressors, they often tried to rebel, causing disruption in production. In contrast, African slaves were torn out of their social groups and transported to foreign lands with little hope for salvation, prompting them to be more obedient. Of course, this does not mean that the African slaves never rebelled, but rather that they did it less often.

Thus, slowly over the course of the 16th century, enslaved African people replaced the natives both as a labor force and, to a degree, as the main population in certain areas. By the mid-17th century, the enslaved African population became a majority in certain areas, like Hispaniola. One might wonder why more Europeans didn't travel to the "New World" to fill in the gap in the workforce, especially since Europe went through a demographic boom after the Black Death, increasing its population. What prevented the exploitation of the local peasantry and poor urban population? A partial answer can be found in the fact that societies had less inclination toward enslaving their own people, coupled with the Christian Church's highly negative stance on the matter. However, it is likely the more crucial fact was that both Spain and Portugal, as well as most other western European nations, underwent an economic expansion. Coupled with that were the constant wars, which required a lot of soldiers. This led to high internal labor demand, leaving no substantial labor force to be sent to the Americas.

The late 16th century saw a slight change in the trade of enslaved Africans. This transformation started in 1580 when Portugal and Spain were united through a personal union, as there was a single king for both nations. This allowed for easier commerce between the Spanish and the Portuguese; however, it also opened up the latter to confrontations with the Dutch. The Dutch, who were fighting the Spanish for their independence, were growing a strong navy, which was used against Portuguese ships and possessions after the union. This was combined with the intrusion of both the British and the French, who began establishing their own presence on the African coast, as well as in the Americas. This slowly led to the Portuguese slave trade monopoly breaking up, as other nations wanted a piece of the profit. Probably the only exception from this were the Spaniards, who, despite having no problem in using slave labor, showed little will to compete in the trade of enslaved people.

Regardless, the Portuguese kept a vital role in the slave trade. Despite being somewhat displaced from other regions, the West African coast remained firmly in their grip. By the early 17th century, with the rise of Brazil as an important sugar manufacturing region, the Portuguese slowly rose both in roles of slave suppliers and of slave importers. In fact, by the 1620s and 1630s, that region managed to surpass the Spanish American dominion as the main slave market. At the same, São Tomé lost its important role in sugar manufacturing due to the rise of Brazil and as a result of Dutch raids, but it became even more significant as a slave-trading hub. Even in the late decades of the 16th century, the enslaved people were directly shipped across the Atlantic, with many using São Tomé as a starting point. The Angolan coast, most notably Luanda, also became more important, as the region grew into a large source of slaves.

Both the rise of Brazil as a slave destination and of Angola as a center of supply can be painted by some raw numbers. Over the course of the 17th century, roughly 560,000 enslaved people were transported to Brazil, with 360,000 being shipped in the latter half, signaling almost a constant rise in the number of poor souls destined for a harsh life on the colonial plantations. According to modern estimates, those numbers represent about 42 percent of the total slave trade in that century. When taking that into account, it should be noted that, geographically speaking, Brazil was far from the largest colonial holding, adding to the weight of the numbers. At the same time, the Angola region supplied roughly between 10,000 and 16,000 people annually over the majority of the 17th century. This means over one million people were imprisoned and sent to servitude from just a single region over the course of only one century.

At the same time, the Portuguese continued to trade for enslaved Africans in Upper Guinea, using Cape Verde as a vital hub, as well as around the Gambia River. They remained the most prolific slave traders over the course of the century, despite having other nations, most notably the Dutch, as competitors. In 1640, Portugal regained independence from Spain, yet it remained the top supplier of enslaved people to the Spanish American domains. In addition, hostilities with the Dutch and other Europeans subsided, although they never fully stopped. The Portuguese also conducted some smaller wars and interventions in the Angola region to secure their positions and influence, making their foothold in Africa the strongest of all the European colonial empires. Yet all those developments in Africa and Europe had less impact on the overall Portuguese slave trade than the following events in Brazil.

Sixteenth-century Portuguese maps of West Africa (top)
and Brazil (bottom). Source: https://commons.wikimedia.org

In the 1690s, the Portuguese discovered substantial sources of gold in Brazil, creating a whole new level of demand for slave labor. The subsequent gold rush was so substantial that Portugal had to ban emigration from its mainland and Atlantic islands to the gold-rich region located about 200 miles (320 kilometers) inland of Rio de Janeiro. Regardless, many Portuguese traveled to Brazil, while many abandoned their plantations in the north of the colony in search of precious metals. Thus began the so-called golden age of Brazil, which, of course, highly benefited Portugal as well. And with it came a slight change in demand for enslaved labor. The southern regions of Brazil saw an increased thirst for African slaves, but unlike the plantation owners of the north, they had a preference for people from the Bight of Benin. They were seen as more superior workers than the Angolans, as well as much more resistant to diseases.

However, the changes in favoring gold over sugar and favoring the Benin coast over Angola as a source of slave labor weren't all-encompassing as it might have seemed in the early decades of the 18th century. The northern regions of Brazil, especially Bahia, diversified from sugar into tobacco and cotton, with the former being important for the slave trade as well. The African traders in the Bight of Benin had developed a "sweet tooth" for tobacco, and they held Bahia in the highest regard, accepting it in barter for enslaved humans. With that, Bahia remained a vital part of the slave trade, often as a connection between the gold mines of southern Brazil and Africa. Along with that, the Portuguese returned to their Angolan preference in the latter 18th century, not only maintaining its earlier quotas of enslaved people but also growing them. Because of that, modern estimates place the entire Angola region as a source of 70 percent of the Portuguese slaves in the 1700s, as well as about 26 percent of the entire Americas.

For the Portuguese, the 18th century was somewhat paradoxical when it came to the slave trade. On the one hand, the central government in Europe began regulating both the taxation and the treatment of enslaved people. With this move, it monetized its gains much more efficiently, taking a percentage of each slave's worth from merchants. It also regulated how many enslaved people could be crammed into a single ship and required proper feeding and at least basic medical care for the slaves. Of course, these laws and measures were empty words on paper more than enacted decisions. In addition, it seems that in mainland Portugal, slavery was growing out of fashion, as slavery was prohibited by 1773. However, Brazil, as well as other colonial holdings, were left unregulated by any slavery laws. That caused a shift toward the Brazilian Portuguese taking the reins of the slave trade. Regardless of such shifts in Portuguese society, the 18th century was most "prolific" for the slave trade, as Portugal reached its highest estimated trafficking count of just above 1.9 million enslaved people.

This paradoxical trend continued into the 19th century, with the Portuguese slowly opting out of the slave trade, although it remained somewhat active in their colonial holdings. In contrast, Brazil gained its independence in 1822, continuing its strong presence in the slave market until the end of the century. It was one of the last Western nations to abolish slavery, doing so in 1888. By then, the combined total of imported enslaved people by the Portuguese and Brazilians reached an estimated 5 million people, or about 40 percent of all slaves brought to the Americas. By the end of the transatlantic slave trade, the Portuguese pioneers remained the most influential European nation in the entire mercantile network of human trafficking. However, for a short while, their Iberian neighbors, the Spaniards, seemed like a prime candidate for the spot. What proved to be the crucial difference?

It seemed that the Spanish Empire would most likely become a leading nation in the slave trade in the early days of colonization. Prior to the Age of Discovery, the Spanish already had legally defined the institution of slavery, and they already had a successful "experiment" on the Canary Islands. Furthermore, it was the Spaniards who first brought slaves to the Americas in 1501, and by 1510, they had started the systematic transportation of enslaved Africans to the continent. In that regard, while the Portuguese were the pioneers of the Atlantic slave trade, at least in regard to the European nations, the Spaniards technically transformed it into the transatlantic slave trade. If that wasn't enough, the Spanish colonial empire was the largest territorially and was the biggest importer of enslaved people in the 16th-century Americas. In those first 100 years, the Spanish colonies bought about 75,000 Africans, being second only to the Portuguese São Tomé. On top of that, the unification with Portugal in 1580 seemed like it would only promulgate the slave trade.

The extent of Atlantic territories of unified Spain and Portugal (top) and 18th-century depiction of social classes in Spanish Mexico, showing Africans only above the natives (bottom). Source: https://commons.wikimedia.org

However, the Spanish never took over the Portuguese when it came to the commerce of human beings. On the one hand, the Spanish never tried nor were able to jeopardize the Portuguese monopoly on the African coast as a source of enslaved labor. This was partially because of the treaty that separated the spheres of colonial control between the two nations but also because of their later unification. Furthermore, although it was possible the Spanish could have overtaken the Portuguese in the early stages of the transatlantic slave trade, when Spain still had the capability to do so, the Spaniards deemed it unnecessary, as the volume of trade was still rather small. The Spanish were focused more on taking control over land in the Americas. Later on, Spain weakened and was unable to interfere, even if there was any will to do so. As such, the Spanish colonies relied upon foreign slave traders to supply them with necessary labor. Initially, they were solely served by the Portuguese, but the Dutch also came during the 17th century, as well as the British and the French.

The Spanish Crown tried to control this supply through the *Asiento de Negros*, a royal license given to merchants for the monopoly over the slave trade to its American dominions. However, this system was flawed and served more for filling the royal treasury than for control over the slave trade. Furthermore, unlike Portugal, whose colonial possessions were small in scope but under a firm grip, Spain had large possessions that were more vulnerable. Spain's naval power and rich treasuries were unrivaled, so it managed to hold on to its colonies. However, after decades of almost constant warfare, something that Portugal tried to avoid, Spain's might began to wane. Soon, its competitors began seizing parts of its domains, like, for example, the French taking parts of Hispaniola, modern-day Haiti, in 1625 or the English conquering Jamaica in 1655. Despite that, the Spanish colonial empire remained substantial, spanning from Mexico to Argentina.

The Spaniards also tried to grow their sugar production, most notably on the Caribbean islands, as well as on the Mexican coast. At the same time, many of their colonies had substantial gold and silver deposits, mainly in southern America. Yet the constant wars had drained the Spanish economy, which meant their colonies also began lagging in development behind the Portuguese, ultimately leading to less need for slave labor. In addition, despite losing large portions of the local indigenous population—in some cases, over 90 percent—what remained of the natives was used more successfully than in Brazil. If nothing else, the Spaniards encountered the developed civilizations of the Maya, the Aztecs, and the Incas, who were more accustomed to large-scale agriculture and more knowledgeable in various crafts. It is vital to point out that the Spanish didn't treat the natives any better than the Africans, making both groups suffer harshly.

All the above-mentioned factors explain why Spain played a lesser part in the transatlantic slave trade, at least when it comes to raw numbers. Regardless, the Spaniards gradually increased their number of bought African slaves. In the 17th century, they reached roughly 300,000, and in the next century, they got up to 580,000. These numbers were still high, but they were nowhere near the Portuguese. Strangely enough, the Spanish slave trade grew in the 19th century, despite the gradual global shift away from slavery, reaching about 700,000 imported enslaved people and the loss of most of its colonial possessions in the early decades of the century. This can be explained by the late development of sugar production in Cuba and Puerto Rico, which received the majority of imported slave labor from the late 18th century onward. Overall, the Spaniards are accountable for about one-sixth of the entire transatlantic slave trade, taking roughly 1.7 million slaves to their colonies over almost four centuries.

It is also interesting to point out that thanks to the vastness of their colonial domains, the Spaniards managed to shift the focal point of their slave imports over the centuries. For example, Hispaniola (modern-day Dominican Republic) initially was a vital point for import, but its grand total was only 30,000, as it was quickly surpassed by the growing importance of Mexico, as well as the unified region of Colombia and Ecuador, which reached about 200,000 each. Other important colonial importers in the 16th and 17th centuries were modern-day Venezuela with 120,000, La Plata (present-day Argentina, Bolivia, and Uruguay) with 100,000, and Peru with 95,000. However, these numbers pale in comparison with the later development of Cuba, a relatively small island that reached a total of about 837,000, as well as tiny Puerto Rico, which imported about 77,000 slaves. Despite that, it's important to remember that no matter where the enslaved Africans were sent, they suffered greatly, and the differences in numbers shouldn't lessen the agony of their experiences.

Overall, the transatlantic pioneers, both in discovery and in the slave trade, proved immensely influential. They set up early merchant routes and systems, developed forced labor systems, and remained constant users of slave labor. In the end, they set an example to other European nations while also having more than a considerable share of the overall number of human beings traded and shipped over the Atlantic. Spain and Portugal together were just shy of an estimated six million traded slaves, which equates to about 56 percent of the total transatlantic slave trade.

Chapter 3 – New Contenders: The Dutch and the French

The Iberian nations were the first in Europe to delve into naval exploration, colonization, and the notorious slave trade. It brought them immense wealth and power, so it wasn't long before other Europeans wanted their share, trying to find their place in the newly bustling economic network. Among the first who managed to challenge the old pioneers were the Dutch.

The Dutch were already quite capable merchants and sailors, with a strong trading network in the North Sea, so they had the tools and knowledge needed to succeed in trade of any kind. However, since the early 16th century, they were under the rule of the Spanish Crown, yet by the 1580s, the Dutch were engaged in a full-blown rebellion, which arose over religious maltreatment. The Spanish Crown fought them with its military and through economic pressure. The Dutch were cut off from Iberian ports, including Lisbon since Portugal had been unified with Spain by this time. Opting to fight back, the Dutch began raiding Spanish ships and colonies. Their initial success caused them to think about threatening the Iberian international trade monopoly. Their focus was mostly set on Asia and the valuable spice trade, which would be led by the now-famous Dutch East India Company (VOC), which was founded in 1602.

The military and economic gains in the East proved more valuable than the Dutch had ever dreamed, causing them to rise as the most important trading nation of the 17th century, overshadowing their Iberian rivals. Swayed by the early success of the VOC, the Dutch decided to form the Dutch West India Company (WIC) in 1621. Unlike the Portuguese and the Spaniards, whose trade was based on individual merchants competing in the same market, the Dutch combined their companies to form an ordered monopoly, increasing their financial capability, efficiency, and military might. In addition, these trading companies weren't only given rights to monopolies but were also allowed to wage wars and sign treaties in the name of the Dutch Republic. To stop the VOC and WIC from clashing, the latter was given the trading monopoly on the West African coast and Americas, while the former kept its business in the East.

The Dutch WIC initially showed no plans or interest in the slave trade. They dealt with more usual resources, like sugar or gold. However, this slowly began to change when they employed their more modern military ships and newer cannons to begin retaking Portuguese colonies. In 1630, the northern part of Brazil, the region of Pernambuco, which was known for its sugar production, fell. The region became known as New Holland, and the Dutch realized they needed African labor to maintain production. This swayed the WIC into engaging in the slave trade, and it soon sailed to Elmina on the Gold Coast, taking it in 1637 from the Portuguese. With that, the Portuguese monopoly was essentially broken, as the Dutch were now able to supply themselves with enslaved labor. From there, they took several smaller Portuguese trading stations on the African coast, culminating in the conquest of Luanda in 1641. The WIC's leaders realized the Angolan slaves were greatly valued by the Brazilian sugar producers, meaning they would bring more profit to the company.

At that moment, it seemed the Dutch were on their way to displace the Portuguese as the owners of the slave trade monopoly. During the 1640s, they managed to become the largest exporters of enslaved people on the Atlantic, as the Portuguese trade network was in shambles. This shift toward human cargo was crowned in 1645 when WIC directors remarked that the slave trade was the soul of the company. However, this success was rather short. By 1648, the Portuguese expelled them from Angola, and in 1654, they retook Brazil. Regardless, the Dutch were determined to remain in the slave trade business. Around 1660, they took control of what was dubbed the Dutch Slave Coast, a region encompassing modern-day Benin, Togo, Ghana, and Nigeria, using it as their main source of enslaved Africans. During the second half of the 17th century, they shifted further away from the idea of reaping the fruits of their own colonies.

A 19th-century painting of the battle that ended the Dutch presence in Brazil. Source: https://commons.wikimedia.org

The Dutch possessions were usually small and had little agricultural potential. Yet they spanned across the Americas, from the Hudson River and New Amsterdam (modern-day New York), across the Netherlands Antilles toward their possessions in the area between the Orinoco and Amazon Rivers, present-day Suriname and Guyana. Because of that, they were best suited for commerce with Spain and

Portugal, as well as with France and England, whose presence in the Caribbean was growing. The Dutch were keen traders, and the WIC directors realized that the French and English were undergoing their own sugar revolution in the region. Since the Dutch had already cracked into the slave trade monopoly of the Portuguese, they were able to offer them the slave labor they needed. At the same time, they exploited the fact that the Spanish had never developed their own supply of enslaved people. By 1674, the WIC's business was almost solely in the commerce of human beings, while the island of Curaçao in the Netherlands Antilles became its largest slave depot.

A 17ᵗʰ-century map of Dutch New Amsterdam and its surrounding territories. Source: https://commons.wikimedia.org

However, the 1660s and 1670s brought crucial change to the Dutch Atlantic trade and the WIC. During these two decades, the company waged two wars against the English, who sought to establish their dominance both on the seas and in all kinds of trade. Over the years of combat, the WIC proved too weak to compete against the new contenders. By 1674, the original WIC dissolved, but it was reestablished the following year as the New West India Company.

The high demand for slaves was enough of an incentive for the Dutch to try again. Yet, by then, it was clear they were losing their place in the slave trade to the British and French; the Portuguese had also managed to recuperate by then. Besides being pushed to the fringes of the slave trade, the wars with England also caused a shift in the geography and use of enslaved labor for the Dutch.

In 1667, under the Treaty of Breda, the Dutch lost their North American possessions to the English but gained some of theirs in Suriname. In their new holdings, the Dutch found already developed sugar production and decided to keep it. For that reason, they no longer solely transported enslaved people, as they began employing forced labor in great numbers. The Dutch Suriname became one of the highest importers in the Dutch slave trade during the 18th century. About two-thirds of the enslaved people were shipped there in the early decades, while this number rose to nearly 90 percent in the later decades. However, by then, the Dutch had lost pace with the other major slave-trading nations despite having some relative rise in quantity, reaching its peak in the mid-18th century. Then came more wars with England and later France, which crumbled what was left of the Dutch slave trade. By 1814, the Dutch had outlawed the commerce of enslaved people, but by then, economic activity in that field had pretty much died out.

The new WIC suffered a similar fate as the Dutch slave trade. It went into a slow decline in the early 18th century, while it lost its slave trade monopoly in the 1730s. The Dutch turned toward free trade, allowing all merchants to participate, probably explaining the overall rise in the number of transported slaves. By 1792, the company was dissolved, with all of its possessions reverting to the Dutch Republic, most notably in Suriname and the Gold Coast, which tried to adapt to an economy without the slave trade.

Generally speaking, the Dutch played an important role in the development of the transatlantic slave trade. They broke the Portuguese monopoly when it seemed impenetrable, allowing other nations to join. They also refined and made the slave trade much more efficient. However, despite that, when talking about raw numbers, the Dutch represented a small percentage of the African slave trade. According to modern estimates, from its start in 1621 to its end in the first decade of the 1800s, the Dutch traders transported somewhere around 530,000 enslaved people. This accounts for about 6 percent of the total transatlantic slave trade. According to other estimates, the Dutch imported roughly around 200,000 African slaves to work on their plantations, mostly in Suriname, which would equate to about 2 percent of all enslaved labor in the Americas. Thus, it is clear that the Dutch Republic's role in the slave trade was more of a supplier than of an employer.

Because of these low numbers, at least when compared to other nations, the Dutch are usually classified as a minor slave-trading nation. There were others who also tried to achieve financial gains in the commerce of human beings, like, for example, the Danish, the Swedish, and the Germans, yet their contribution and impact were rather small and less important in the overall picture. For this reason, their role in the transatlantic slave trade won't be touched upon in any greater detail. Unlike them, and in quite a different manner than the Dutch, the French played a major role in the slave trade.

France exhibited an early interest in entering the overall trade monopoly with Spain and Portugal, as far back as the late 15th century. However, it wasn't able to penetrate it since the Iberians were at the height of their power. Nonetheless, the French continued to prod and poke both in Africa and in the Americas. They found initial success in modern-day Canada. The French explored it throughout the 16th century but only managed to colonize it in the early years of the 17th century. Yet this region wasn't as valuable as the southern colonies, as its climate wasn't suited for sugar growing. For this reason, Canada never became an importer of slaves, having less than 2,000 enslaved Africans through the entirety of the transatlantic slave trade. A more important foothold was achieved in the Caribbean, where during the 1620s and 1630s, the French managed to gain control of what was to become the French West Indies, most notably the islands of Martinique and Guadeloupe. Farther south, the French attempted to settle what is today French Guiana; however, their initial attempts were unsuccessful, becoming an operating colony only in the 1660s.

With the establishment of the Caribbean colonies, the French entered both into the sugar production and slave trade. In 1642, a royal decree legalized the slave trade in France, marking its official entry into the commerce of humans. However, they initially relied on using other Europeans as their supplier and bought a relatively small number of enslaved Africans. Their main supplier was the Dutch, creating a somewhat strong relationship with them. The French colonies, mainly Martinique, depended on the Dutch for much-needed slave labor, yet the overall economic policy of 17th-century France was one of self-sufficiency in all aspects. Like many other European nations of that time, one of the ways to achieve that was to maximize exports and minimize imports, an economic doctrine known as mercantilism. Thus, their dependency on the Dutch became a thorn in France's side. This idea of economic independence was pushed to the forefront of French national interests in the second half of the 17th century under the rule of King Louis XIV and Prime Minister Jean-Baptiste Colbert.

One of the first steps they made in pursuit of that goal in their American colonial domain was to expand it. Their most important gain was Saint-Domingue, the western part of Hispaniola, modern-day Haiti. By the mid-16th century, it was a largely overlooked Spanish colony, as it was plagued by pirates. The French conquest of Saint-Domingue began from the island of Tortuga, which was incorporated into the French colonies in 1659. By 1665, the conquest of Saint-Domingue was complete, giving the French much-needed fertile land for growing sugar. The Spanish never fully recognized the loss of their territory, but they tacitly accepted the new power on Hispaniola. Soon, Saint-Domingue became the largest French importer of enslaved people, overtaking Martinique by the end of the century.

However, expanding the American domains to increase gains from the colonies was only part of the mercantilist French plans, as they were still largely dependent on the Dutch slave trade. Their first step to counter this issue was to establish a foothold in Africa, which was achieved in 1659 when a trading post named Saint-Louis was established on the island located near the mouth of the Senegal River. During the 1660s, France was obliged by a treaty to aid the Dutch against the English, something Louis wanted to avoid as much as possible. When that failed, he kept French involvement to a minimum. By 1672, he had turned against the Dutch, waging a new war that lasted six years and left France with important gains for its slave trade. In the Caribbean, it gained the island of Tobago, and in Africa, their domain grew to include the slave-trading posts of Gorée and Arguin, allowing for wider trade within the Senegambia region. Additionally, the Dutch were banned from trading within the French West Indies. The volume of the French slave trade increased after these victories, as it was less dependent on its economic contenders.

A 19ʰ-century French painting depicting the slave trade on the West African coast. Source: https://commons.wikimedia.org

France's attempts to gain self-sufficiency wasn't only accomplished by conquering new lands and trading posts. Since the early 17th century, the French had tried to copy Dutch success by creating trading companies with various rights and monopiles given by the government. The most serious and largest attempt came in 1664 when the French West India Company was formed. It was given a monopoly over all trade in the Americas, from Canada to French Guiana, including the slave trade. Yet despite having the full backing of the state, by 1674, the company had dissolved and was succeeded by other smaller local companies, like the Company of Senegal. Its failure was partially caused by the clashes with the English and the Dutch, and it set a precedent for French companies lasting only a few years before being dissolved. As a result of these failures, and despite all the effort, French traders didn't succeed in satisfying the need for slave labor on their sugar plantations, often forcing them to look at other nations for additional imports.

Nonetheless, the French managed to rise up as a slave-trading nation. In the last quarter of the century, its ships transported about 2,000 enslaved people annually, roughly as much as the Dutch, yet much fewer than the Portuguese and English, who both went as high as 7,000. In contrast, French imports exploded in the same period, with about 71,000 slaves being brought to Saint-Domingue and about 42,000 to Martinique. This late rise of Saint-Domingue as a sugar producer was enough for it to reach almost 50 percent of 16th-century France's import of slaves, though it was closely followed by Martinique. Overall, during the century, France's dominions imported about 155,000 slaves, a number far behind the Spanish and the Portuguese, yet its territories were considerably smaller (as long as Canada is excluded from the comparison).

Regardless of their questionable success when compared to the leading slave-trading nations, the French were growing, as did the overall market for enslaved people. Together with the English, they managed to oust the Dutch, but by the last years of the century, these two new colonial powers began struggling for maritime control over the Atlantic trade. Their full-blown clashes began in 1689 and lasted until 1713, with a short hiatus from 1697 to 1702. These were, in fact, two large European conflicts, where several allied nations combated against the rising power of France. The English were only one of many who fought them; however, in terms of the Atlantic theater of war, they were the most important the French fought. On top of that, the French also fought against the Spanish and the Dutch, who, despite seeing a decrease in their power, were still formidable foes.

French forces saw heavy losses in Europe yet proved remarkable both in the Caribbean and on the African coast. French privateers raided English and Spanish ships, as well as their colonies. Most notable were their invasions of Jamaica, the center of English colonial power at the time. These victories helped French slave traders, as it secured their positions both in Africa and the Americas. France, through its dynastic influence, obtained the *Asiento* from the Spanish in 1701, becoming the sole supplier of enslaved people for the oldest and still the largest domain in the Americas. This was part of France's attempt to meddle with the succession of the Spanish Crown, possibly leading to a union of the two states. It was enough to reignite the briefly paused war. The successes on the Atlantic front continued, but in the end, the losses in Europe meant that France lost all its gains during the wars, including the *Asiento*, weakening its position both as a naval power and as a leading slave-trading nation.

Despite the defeats on the battlefield, the French colonies continued to grow and develop. Saint Domingue was one of the leading sugar producers in the Caribbean, furthering the need for an imported labor force. Furthermore, France managed to expand its possessions on the American mainland. Though it had been exploring and attempting to settle the region of Louisiana since the 1660s, it only became a fully functioning French colony in the last decade of the century. There, the French faced a similar problem as most other European colonizers: the lack of a workforce. The main products were tobacco and cotton, which, like sugar, required a lot of labor to be cost effective. Thus, by 1699, the French started importing slaves in that region as well, adding yet another destination for their merchants. Furthermore, French Guiana was also expanding, seeking slave labor for its further development. However, both of these colonies were small-scale importers of slave labor compared to the sugar-producing islands.

The growth of enslaved people, as well as the rising volume of the slave trade in French colonies throughout the late 17th and early 18th centuries, prompted the government in Paris to legally regulate this aspect of colonial life. After years of preparation, *Code Noir* was issued in 1685, and over the next several years, it was slowly adopted and applied across the French West Indies. These laws regulated the treatment of slaves, their position in regards to the law, and their rights if they were freed. However, the intention of these laws wasn't aimed at improving a slave's life, despite having articles pertaining to the issue. Their sole goal was to legally control the slave trade and, through it, secure both sugar production and French sovereignty over the colonies. As such, many slave masters ignored the articles concerning corporal punishment, which were regulated by the law, continuing their atrocities against the enslaved. *Code Noir* was later revised in 1723 and 1724, and it remained the main legal framework of slavery in the French Caribbean domain throughout the 18th century.

Due to the arrival of peace among the European colonial empires after 1713, sugar production and trade continued to develop. The French colonies, most notably Saint Domingue, began producing coffee, creating another export. By then, this colony became known as the "Pearl of the Antilles." Other French colonies prospered as well, but most of them faced a similar setback. Neither the French mainland nor Canada provided them with enough supplies, most notably foodstuffs, timber, working animals, and slaves. Thus, French colonists turned toward their British neighbors, selling their sugar and sugar products, like rum and molasses. Soon, the British sugar producers felt threatened by the advances of the French on their market. This caused the British Parliament in London to issue duties and bans on the import of French sugar in 1733, but this was not rigorously enforced in the beginning. The competition in sugar production contributed to the slowly increasing tension between the two nations, which would soon boil over.

First, the English went to war with Spain in 1739, with France allying with the latter in 1744. In return, it was given the *Asiento*, boosting the French slave trade for a short time. However, the English soon mastered the Atlantic Ocean and used their naval supremacy to cut off the French colonies. This hurt both sugar production and the slave trade. Official peace was secured in 1748, with little change in the Atlantic territories. The English regained the *Asiento*, while the French islands returned to the slave trade and sugar exports. Regardless, over the next several years, both sides sought to gain the upper hand. Their main goal was to achieve economic primacy, causing the two nations to clash over the slave trade as well. Both competed over furthering their control over the African mainland, most notably the Gold Coast. By 1750, the British had abandoned their *Asiento*, which once again reverted to France. Thanks to a fragile peace and the *Asiento*, the French slave trade and sugar production flourished.

A painting depicting a naval battle between France and Britain in the 18ᵗʰ century. Source: https://commons.wikimedia.org

However, by 1756, another war had erupted between the two largest European colonial powers. Yet, once again, their struggle caught other nations in the whirlwind, most notably Spain. The war lasted until 1763, ending with a victory for England and its allies. Throughout the conflict, the British proved to be militarily superior, conquering all of France's colonial possessions in the Caribbean except for Saint Domingue. Furthermore, they also took over their holdings in Senegal, including Gorée. At that moment, it seemed that dark clouds loomed over the French slave trade and sugar production. However, France managed to conquer the Mediterranean island of Minorca from the British early in the war, which was important to their enemies. This allowed them to bargain for the return of Martinique and Guadeloupe in 1763, as well as Gorée. However, all other North American colonies were lost. Canada, save a single island of its coast, went to the British, while Louisiana was handed over to Spain.

Nevertheless, these losses proved mostly irrelevant for the slave trade. The North American territories weren't large importers of forced labor. Furthermore, sugar production on Guadeloupe and Martinique only expanded under the English, who continued to ship slaves onto the briefly held islands. During the peace, the sugar industry in Saint Domingue exploded. This colony alone produced as much as the entire British American domain. The French Indies entered their golden age, with both quality and quantity, resulting in the number of imported enslaved workers growing as well. Once again, the French were unable to satisfy their own demand, turning to their British competitors for additional slaves along with other needed resources. However, this trade wasn't localized solely on the Caribbean islands, as trade between the French West Indies and the British American colonies had expanded in the years following the war. Furthermore, the French began developing agricultural production in French Guiana, though it was still far from becoming the prized Pearl of the Antilles.

The peace lasted until 1778, for France decided to stand alongside the American revolutionaries in their struggle against Britain. Their decision to aid the Americans was twofold. The Thirteen Colonies became important economic partners to the French, and the French also wanted to enact revenge for their previous defeat. While the English were more focused on the continental front, the French won several victories in the Caribbean, conquering several smaller islands there. Additionally, they had some initial success in Senegal as well. They retook Saint-Louis and razed the Fort St. James. However, the English occupied Gorée later on. This time, France had the upper hand in the peace talks, which had been furthered by the American victory in the revolution. Thus, when the Treaty of Paris of 1783 came about, France could postulate its demands. France's principal goal was to regain control over the Senegal region, as it was vital to its increasing thirst for slave labor. Britain accepted, and the two nations also signed trade agreements, allowing the British traders to trade for gum in the region.

Along with consolidating the Senegalese coast, the French gained the island of Tobago. This was yet another sugar-producing colony, which was also in need of slave labor. France focused on expanding both its sugar production and its slave trade. Firstly, a new breed of sugarcane was introduced to the colonies. Its yields per acre were about three times higher than the British. Furthermore, trade regulations were liberalized, which was more important for the commerce of humans, while new trading companies were also formed. Because of these changes, French merchants rushed to the colonies, seeking to get rich quickly. The 1780s became a decade of great expansion for the French colonies. Their sugar production doubled, as well as its slave imports. From 1783 to 1793, the French slave traders brought an average of almost 30,000 enslaved annually. However, this expansion didn't last long.

The French mainland, despite the bustling sugar and slave trade in the colonies, was descending into a social and economic crisis. This led to the famous French Revolution in 1789, causing great struggles among the European powers in 1792. It wasn't long before these clashes manifested on the seas as well. However, the most significant defeat and loss for the French colonial empire didn't come from the hands of other Europeans—it actually came from a slave revolt. For the majority of the century, Saint Domingue was infamous for its harsh treatment of the enslaved people. The arrival of revolutionary ideals, most notably liberty and equality, brought false hope for the enslaved. Their hopes for freedom were declined, and they also faced the possibility of an even harsher regime, as some of the slave owners thought about seceding from revolutionary France. In 1791, the slaves rebelled.

Illustration of the 1791 slave rebellion in Saint Domingue.
Source: https://commons.wikimedia.org

Over the next thirteen years, the slave uprising faced many enemies, including Britain and Spain. Despite being enemies of France, both of these nations feared the revolt would spread to their territories; also, the control of Saint Domingue would give them an upper hand against the French. Regardless, the rebellion persevered, defeating wave after wave of European forces, including Napoleon Bonaparte's invasion in 1802. Thus, on January 1804, Saint Domingue proclaimed independence and changed its name to Haiti. Slavery was abolished there, but its effects on the global abolitionary movement are still disputed by modern historians. Regardless, while still struggling to maintain its colonial empire, France abolished slavery in 1794. This act was reversed by Napoleon but to little effect, as the war was still raging. After the French defeat in 1815, the new government promised to abolish slavery, but this was only enacted in 1826.

Despite the issue of legality, which wasn't always enforced in the colonial domains, the slave trade in France had been destroyed, for the most part, by 1793. By then, the French had secured their position in history as the fourth largest slave-trading nation. Between 1700 and 1793, French merchants boarded slightly more than one million enslaved Africans onto their ships. During that period, the vast majority of them were sent to Saint Domingue, roughly 750,000 people or about 75 percent of France's entire import, making it the largest importer of slaves in the Caribbean. Martinique followed with about 125,000, while Guadeloupe took in about 40,000. French Guiana and Louisiana together fell short of 20,000. Overall, it is estimated that the French imported about 15 percent of the entire Atlantic slave trade up to the year 1800, with the percentage falling to about 13 percent if the 19th century is counted. Speaking in terms of crude numbers, throughout the entirety of its participation in the slave trade, France took about 1.4 million enslaved people from Africa, though less than 1.2 million arrived to the American continent. Many perished on their journey across the ocean.

The majority of Africans came from western-central Africa, roughly 36 percent, and the Bight of Benin, which supplied slightly less than 25 percent. This is slightly surprising since France only focused on building colonies on the Senegalese coast. The Senegambian region accounted for only about 6.5 percent of the French slave trade. Because of this, the French rarely represented a majority in any region's slave exports. The focus of French merchants depended on the current state of political and economic affairs, both in Africa and the Caribbean, as well as among the Europeans themselves. These also affected the temporal distribution of French trade, especially during the 18th century. It was characterized by downfalls during the wars and peaks during peacetime, each of which would be higher than the last. The last one, between 1780 and 1793, accounted for about one-third of the entire slave trade that century. In those thirteen years, about 300,000 Africans were shipped by the French, reaching a record of about 41,000 in a single year in that period.

As such, the French secured their place in the infamous history of the Atlantic slave trade as the fourth largest slave-trading nation. Together with the Dutch, they penetrated the Iberian monopoly on the commerce of human beings, albeit in two largely different ways. While the Dutch sought to supply others, without using much of the slaves themselves, the French tried to make a self-sufficient slave network of their own. Regardless of the differences, both left significant marks on the transatlantic slave trade.

Chapter 4 – English Ascendancy to the Top of the Slave Trade

Due to the Spanish demand for slaves, the Portuguese established the transatlantic slave trade. Their grip on it was tight for over a century. Then the Dutch disputed the Iberian monopoly while the French tried to find their own place in the slave trade network. However, it was the English who managed to oust the Portuguese from their top spot in the commerce of humans.

While the Iberians were still commanding the sea in the 16th century, the English were trying to find their place among the colonial empires. At the time, England still wasn't a major naval power, so its possibilities in the Americas were limited. Their focus was set on North America, where the Iberians had little interest. Some early expeditions and claims were made in the regions of Newfoundland, Virginia, and other regions of the East Coast of the modern-day US. Yet, no permanent settlements were made for quite some time, with one of their most famous failures being the Roanoke colony in the 1580s. Since they had no colonies and lacked the capability to compete with the Spanish and Portuguese fleets, the English had little incentive to dabble in the slave trade during the 16th century.

However, there was a notable exception: John Hawkins. He was an English privateer, backed by the Crown, who realized there was profit to be made by trading enslaved humans. Between 1562 and 1567, he made three voyages from Africa, specifically the Sierra Leone region, where he captured several hundred Africans and participated in a local war, to the Spanish colonies in Hispaniola and Venezuela. This early attempt to actively participate in the slave trade was cut short by Hawkins's defeat in 1567, with him barely escaping alive. He lost all his gains, and with that, the English lost their interest in the profits of the slave trade. For the next roughly seventy-five years, they had little to do with slavery. In the 1620s, an English trader refused to deal with slaves when offered by his African partner. He said that neither he nor the English dealt with the trade of human beings. However, change was already on the horizon. In 1607, the English established their first successful American colony in Jamestown. Others soon followed, most importantly the early Caribbean colonies of Saint Kitts, Barbados, and Nevis in the 1620s. The English started producing tobacco on the North American mainland and sugar on the Caribbean isles.

The so-called "Sugar Revolution," which marks the beginning of English orientation toward slavery in its colonies, was actually brought on by the Dutch. Their traders first brought sugarcane to Barbados in 1640 from Brazil, which they occupied at the time. Their idea was to act as middlemen traders with the English, supplying slaves while exporting sugar to Europe. Yet the Dutch plans failed. While the English quickly adopted sugar as their main product in the West Indies, they initially relied on white indentured labor, as well as people fleeing the English Civil War. Prisoners also made a significant portion of the workforce in early English colonies. At the same time, sugar production was still on a small scale, further diminishing Dutch revenue.

However, change came quickly. The English were aware that they were losing profit to the Dutch, and in 1651, British Parliament banned foreign ships from trading in their colonies. At the same time, the Guinea Company, which was founded in 1618 for conventional trading along the African coast, reoriented itself toward the commerce of humans. They sought to fulfill the growing demand on Barbados, which by then had roughly an equal number of African slaves and white Englishmen of various social status working on sugar plantations. This led to growing competition with the Dutch traders, yet relations remained peaceful though strained. It is vital to mention that prior to the 1650s, the English traders had some dealings with humans as a commodity. However, it was on a minute scale and more of an exception than the rule. The records about it are scant, reinforcing the notion that early 17th-century English merchants weren't greatly involved with the slave trade.

A 17th-century map of Jamaica. Source: https://commons.wikimedia.org

Another important development was the enlargement of the English West Indies. In 1648, England began colonizing the Bahamas, which was finalized by 1666. More importantly, England took Jamaica from the Spanish in 1655. The latter began steadily shifting focus toward sugar production, opening yet another slave market for the English merchants. Yet, like Barbados, initial demand was low. Firstly, the Spanish left some of their African slaves, while the English sought to fulfill labor force demands by bringing white indentured workers. The English also expanded their colonies on the North American mainland as well, for example, founding Maryland, Massachusetts, and Carolina, though the latter wasn't properly settled until 1670. These colonies also depended more on the English colonists and the servants they brought than the African slaves, yet slavery was present there since their early days. For example, in 1638 in Maryland, there were proposed bills concerning the exemption of slaves from Christian rights, which were shared by both freemen and their indentured servants. Regardless, the import of slaves in these early years, both to the American mainland and the Caribbean isles, was more in the realms of hundreds than thousands.

The growth of England's colonial domain only expanded the demand for enslaved labor. This gave an increased incentive to the traders to challenge the Dutch, their primary suppliers, in that field. The English Crown, which had been restored in 1660 after the fall of Cromwell's republic, realized the only viable solution was to establish a trading company. Thus, in 1663, the Company of Royal Adventurers Trading into Africa was formed, with its aim to trade both in human beings and other precious goods like gold or ivory. The newly founded company's initial goal was to secure trading stations on the African coast. They either founded their own or conquered existing forts from their competitors. Their most notable advance came between 1665 and 1667 during the war with the Dutch, which had been sparked by their economic competition with each other. However, the English lost the war and had to pay indemnities. Yet their loss wasn't complete. In Africa, they secured a loose network of forts and trading posts, stretching from the Senegambia to Benin, with Cape Coast Castle in Ghana being the most notable.

Furthermore, they gained New Amsterdam, or New York as it is known today.

Nevertheless, the war proved too costly for the company. It was an expensive endeavor, and for those roughly two years, trade was virtually nonexistent. After the war, the Royal Adventurers tried to sublet their monopoly to free merchants in an attempt to recuperate, but by 1672, it had reorganized into the new Royal African Company. It was granted a broader monopoly and more rights than the Adventurers Company had, as it had the right to enforce laws, occupy non-Christian lands, sign treaties with non-European nations, and more. It seems the new company was given free rein to deal with anything besides involving England in wars with its European competitors. As before, the slave trade was one of its principal aims, as the thirst for an enslaved workforce continued to grow in the Caribbean colonies. The Royal African Company traded on the entire African coast, from Senegal to Angola, trying not to limit its focus on a singular region. However, its main sources of slaves came from the regions of the Bight of Benin and Bight of Biafra, constituting over 55 percent of the English slaves exported until 1689.

The Royal African Company initially had a great start. Until the war with France in 1689, the company transported more than 100,000 African slaves across the Atlantic, averaging more than 6,000 people annually. At its peak, it transported more than 8,000 enslaved in a single year. The main destination for the English traders was Barbados, which took in about 40 percent of the trafficked Africans. This was partially due to its more developed sugar production but also because the island was where the English would first land when sailing from Africa. Furthermore, many of its planters were also shareholders in the company.

Barbados was closely followed by Jamaica, which was slowly expanding as a sugar production center, taking in about 30 percent of the enslaved. About 10 percent of the slaves were shipped to Nevis, while other colonies, including Virginia and Maryland, were only minor importers, despite slowly expanding tobacco and cotton production. It is also important to note that modern historians estimate that during the 1680s, one in four Africans lost their lives while on their way to the Americas. Another interesting piece of information is that the English sugar producers in the colonies, unlike their counterparts in Brazil, preferred to have their slaves from Guinea rather than from Angola. In contrast to the Portuguese, they valued docility and compliance more than the capability to endure harsh conditions and labor.

The relations between the planters and the company quickly deteriorated. Many of the sugar producers began complaining about its monopoly, claiming they kept their prices high while still not being able to satisfy the demand for forced labor. Furthermore, some of them even complained that the enslaved were of poor quality. This only adds another layer to the picture of how rough conditions were for the African slaves, as well as how the English and other European colonists saw the enslaved as mere commodities and not as human beings. These complaints also depict the growing trouble the Royal African Company had been facing since the 1680s. Sugar prices were dropping, cutting down its profits, while illegal traders began to encroach on its monopoly. Furthermore, it was obliged to pay for the upkeep of English settlements on the African coast while many of the planters increased their debts to the company.

These issues continued to pile up, and they weighed down the company. Further problems came in 1688, with the onset of the Glorious Revolution, which essentially voided the official monopoly of the Royal African Company. Then, in 1689, the war with France ensued, causing additional disturbances to trade. In 1690, the company appealed to British Parliament to have its monopoly reaffirmed in an attempt to save its business, at least to some degree, yet its pleas were futile. At the end of the war in 1697, the Royal African Company reported enormous financial losses. Its proponents tried to argue that the African trade was beneficial to the entire

English kingdom and that the forts were necessary to maintain its trade network. This led Parliament to find a compromise between the company and the free traders. In 1698, it passed an act that allowed all merchants to trade on the African coast, although those not belonging to the company had to pay a 10 percent fee. This tax was given to the company for the upkeep of fortifications, and in return, they were obliged to provide protection to all English traders who were in need.

Map of British Atlantic possessions around 1700.
Source: https://commons.wikimedia.org

However, this came too late. The Royal African Company was already in decline. In the decade between 1690 and 1700, free traders transported almost 38,000 slaves, while the company reached slightly more than 25,000. The company continued to lobby for the return of its monopoly after the compromise, causing the English government to perform an inquiry into its claim that the free slave trade would cause overall losses. Their results contradicted the company's claims. In less than a decade, the overall English slave trade had reached 93,000 enslaved people exported to the Americas, with about 75,000 coming from the free traders. Even at its peak during the monopoly era, the Royal African Company had exported less than this. However, the free merchants weren't the only beneficiaries of this expansion to the slave trade, as planters in the Americas had access to the labor force they needed to expand their production.

The most notable increase was in Jamaica, which was the destination for almost 50 percent of the imported slaves. Out of those, almost 36,000 came from private traders, while the company supplied less than 7,000 enslaved Africans. This shift toward free trade also benefited Virginia and Maryland, which had been largely neglected by the company. Combined, these mainland colonies now received almost 10 percent of the imported slaves. In 1712, the act of compromise expired, and it wasn't extended. British Parliament was persuaded that the free slave trade was better for the further expansion of both trade and for plantations and production. The company continued to partake in the slave trade for another two decades, yet their annual numbers averaged below 1,000 transported Africans. Afterward, the company dealt with ivory and gold before going defunct in the 1750s. However, the overall commerce of human beings among English traders continued to expand and grow.

Before moving on to explain and describe the golden age of the English slave trade, it is vital to take a step back and look at the legal aspect of slavery in this nation. Unlike the French or the Portuguese, the English never created a unified code of laws regarding slavery. Many opposed the very idea of it as being non-English in nature. Of course, this didn't prohibit some of them to exploit it for their own gain. Nevertheless, the rise of slavery in the second half of the 16th century demanded some legal basis for it, if nothing else than to protect the English planters' property. This was the base idea of the Barbados Slave Code, which was passed in 1661 and stipulated that the slaves were to be protected by law as any other good. With this, the enslaved were legally represented as property, not human beings. This, in turn, meant that the slaves were denied basic rights, like the right to life, which was guaranteed by English common law. The enslaved were left completely at the mercy of their masters, who could do with them as they pleased.

Unlike codes passed by other European slave-trading nations, the Barbados Code doesn't deal with the upkeep of slaves besides requiring their masters to provide them with a single set of clothes each year. Housing, food, working conditions, and any other aspect of the slaves' lives weren't mentioned, further adding to the inhumane treatment of the enslaved. Unfortunately, this code became the basis for all other English colonies and their slave laws. Similar codices were adopted across the English dominion, for example, in Jamaica (1664), South Carolina (1696), and Antigua (1702). Despite being based on the Barbados Slave Code, all of these colonies tweaked their laws to suit their needs; for example, in early Jamaican slavery laws, the death penalty was more sparsely proscribed due to the poor supply of slaves. Over time, these codes were slightly changed, yet their essence remained largely the same.

It is also significant to note that slave laws were passed in Virginia at around the same as Barbados. Unlike in other colonies, those laws were not fully based on the Barbados Code; though, due to its close ties with the Caribbean colonies, some parts were at least inspired by it. Those set of laws became a unified code in 1705. The Virginia Slave Codes became a model for other tobacco colonies, like Maryland, Delaware, and North Carolina. However, these laws didn't really involve the treatment of the slaves. They were more aimed at legalizing the slave trade and establishing greater control over the rising African population. This was achieved by segregation and the dehumanization of the enslaved people. These codes also show how slavery expanded through the English colonies, both geographically and through time.

Overall, during the 17th century, modern estimates put the volume of the English slave trade at about 330,000 people. Most of these, about 300,000, came in the second half of the century. The sharpest increase came after 1680, as the last two decades of the century saw about 50 percent of the overall English slave trade. England went from being basically noninvolved in the slave trade to only falling short of the Portuguese in about a century. However, it was merely the beginning, as the 18th century saw the English dominate the transatlantic slave trade. There were several reasons behind this expansion. As it was already mentioned, part of the success came from the liberalization of the slave trade, as well as of all other merchant branches. More capital, more competition, and most importantly, more traders meant more business.

Yet the 18th-century expansion of the English slave trade wasn't solely the result of said liberalization. Another notable influence came from strengthening British naval power and dominance. Despite still being challenged by the French and, to a much lesser degree, the Dutch, the English became the most powerful nation on the seas. This allowed it to expand its merchant fleet and broaden its reach while carrying more cargo than before. Of course, part of this came with overall naval developments, as European ships grew in size. Coupled with the ability to acquire and transport more enslaved people was the fact that the American slave market was constantly growing, fueled by the constant thirst for more production and financial gain. Unlike in the previous century, when expanding the slave market was primarily the result of acquiring new colonial domains, the British 18th-century slave market was mainly growing because the existing colonies needed an ever-increasing number of slaves to sustain their growing production. The most notable example of this was Jamaica, which became both the biggest importer of enslaved people as well as the largest producer of sugar in the British American colonies.

However, this doesn't mean the British colonial domain didn't expand. After the War of the Spanish Succession, also known as Queen Anne's War, which ended in 1713, Great Britain was awarded Newfoundland and the Hudson Bay region in modern-day Canada, as well as Saint Kitts in the Caribbean. By 1732, Georgia was founded, which was the last of the Thirteen Colonies, while other mainland colonies expanded and grew. However, the biggest expansion came after the Seven Years' War, which was concluded with the Treaty of Paris in 1763. With this significant victory, Britain was allowed to keep control of Canada, Grenada, Tobago, Saint Vincent, and Dominica while also gaining the eastern half of French Louisiana, encompassing the area from the Appalachian Mountains to the banks of the Mississippi River. Small gains were achieved in the Senegambian region as well. British fortunes soon reversed with their defeat in the American Revolutionary War (1775-1783). It lost the Thirteen Colonies, as they proclaimed their independence, while France regained some of the lost Senegambian ports and Tobago. Finally, with the French Revolutionary Wars in the last decade of the century, the British gained control over French Guiana in 1797, as well as both Trinidad and Tobago in 1802.

Nonetheless, these territorial changes were of less consequence for the slave trade. Canada was economically unsuited for the use of forced labor. The aforementioned Caribbean islands were small; even though they engaged in sugar production, their overall impact on the increase of imported slaves cannot be considered a driving force for the growth of the English slave trade. Only Grenada and Dominica had more substantial slave imports in the second half of the century, which was quite high in raw numbers; combined, they imported slightly more than 220,000 between 1750 and 1800. French Guiana also presented a potential market for the export of enslaved Africans, yet this region, like Trinidad and Tobago, was under British control for a short time before slavery was abolished. Thus, their impact on the English slave trade was also marginal, though not nonexistent.

A similar judgment could be passed about the expansion of the Thirteen Colonies. There was reasonable growth, both in claimed and factually settled lands throughout the 18th century, and this enlargement somewhat expanded the slave market, especially in the southern states, whose climate was suitable for cash crops like tobacco, cotton, and rice. However, most of these territorial expansions either weren't in the regions suitable for the cultivation of cash crops, or those areas weren't fully settled or exploited. Nevertheless, there was a clear increase in the need for enslaved labor in the American colonies. Furthermore, the overall volume of the English slave trade continued to grow even after the US declared independence, clearly indicating that the North American mainland still hadn't become a vital market for the English slave traders.

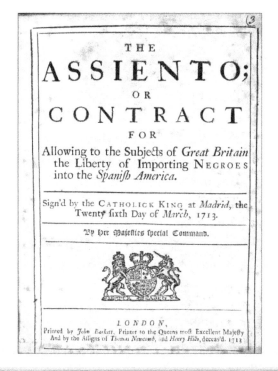

There was yet another aspect that expanded the scope of the English slave trade. Throughout the 18th century, many British merchants supplied foreign markets as well. After the peace of 1713, their traders were given the Spanish *Asiento*. However, this proved to be less lucrative than the English were perhaps hoping. The frequent wars often paused this trade agreement, and even when it was active, the Spanish weren't in much need of slave labor. It was only in the late 18th century, with the rise of sugar production in Cuba, that the English traders saw an increase in the Spanish demand. By the early 19th century and with the abolition of the slave trade in Britain, the English supplied around 95,000 enslaved people to the Spanish, mostly to their Cuban colonies. Another notable foreign market was, surprisingly, the French West Indies. Despite the frequent wars and overall competition, it seems the French planters turned to their enemies when their own traders were unable to supply them with needed forced labor. Over the 18th century and the early years of the 19th century, the English transported about 85,000 African slaves to the French. Their main destinations were Martinique and Guadeloupe.

When it comes to the issue of where the English took their slaves from, the numbers provide a clear favorite. From the start of the liberalized slave trade in 1690 until 1807, almost 36 percent of the enslaved people exported by the British traders came from the Bight of Biafra. The percentage actually grew throughout this period, as the Biafra region, at some point, accounted for roughly 40 percent of the slaves taken by the English. It was followed by the Gold Coast with almost 20 percent and western-central Africa with about 17 percent. The latter remained the same percentage throughout the century, while the Gold Coast lowered its exports. The Bight of Benin had a similar trajectory, going from about 14 percent to just 6 percent, as did the Senegambian region, which dropped from 9 percent to 5 percent. Besides the Biafra region, only the Sierra Leone and the Windward coast, the modern-day Ivory Coast, saw an increase in their participation in the English slave trade. The former went from just about 2 percent to about 7 percent, while the latter increased its share from 5 percent to 8 percent.

Finally, there is the question of temporal distribution and the evolution of the English slave trade throughout the 18th century. Overall, throughout almost the whole period, the volume of human beings shipped over the Atlantic by the British consistently grew. However, there were some notable periods of more concentrated expansions, as well as some dipping points. The first notable period of growth for the English slave trade was in the early 1700s when the English achieved an annual average of between 12,000 to 14,000 trafficked Africans. This expansion continued to rise until the 1740s. The war with France temporarily reduced the British commerce of human beings, which fell about 20 to 25 percent. However, the increase in volume continued to rise after the conflict and throughout the 1750s. The Seven Years' War slowed down this growth, yet no significant drop was made, and it continued to expand, reaching an annual rate of about 27,000 by 1763.

The English slave trade reached a new high in the early 1770s, but the American Revolutionary War caused yet another major drop. Almost all trade to the American mainland halted, while the British lost more than 50 percent of its volume of transported slaves. Nevertheless, the British slave trade quickly recovered. By the 1790s, it had reached a peak of almost 40,000 slaves in a single year. In fact, from 1780 up to the ban of the slave trade, the English trafficked almost one million Africans. To put this in perspective, in 1801, the entirety of Great Britain had a population of about 10.5 million people. It is also worth noting that between 1791 and 1807, the English accounted for about 52 percent of the entire volume of the transatlantic slave trade. Alongside the revival of the British slave trade, the merchants based in the newly formed United States also quickly returned to business. According to some estimates, in the period since their independence in 1783 until the enactment of the slave-trading ban in 1808, the American traders brought about 150,000 Africans to the American continent.

However, only about 60,000 of those were brought to the United States. This was partially due to several states banning the import of enslaved people, although they did not ban the slave trade in general. Nevertheless, the American traders found other markets for the enslaved people they brought from Africa. The most significant was Cuba, but they also shipped to other Spanish colonies. Other markets they supplied were Martinique and Guadeloupe, occasionally taking advantage of the occasional wars between the French and the British. With that, the US slave trade became third in regards to volume in the early years of the 19th century. They averaged about 14 percent of the entire trade, falling only behind the British and Portuguese. Yet, regardless of their official independence, the American slave traders were largely part of the English network, as many of them once sailed under the British flag. They continued to work in accordance with the general outline of the English slave trade. For these reasons, as well as the fact that the independent US slave trade lasted for less than three decades, its contribution will be added to the English slave trade in the final calculation.

A painting of 19ᵗʰ-century slave traders in the southern US.
Source: https://commons.wikimedia.org

Finally, there is the question of where the majority of the enslaved trafficked by the English ended up. In this aspect, Jamaica was far ahead of any other British colony, as it took in about 39 percent of all the enslaved people imported by the English, which equates to roughly 928,000 people in the span of slightly more than a century. It was closely followed by Barbados, where around 311,000 enslaved people ended up. The combined accumulative number for the entire United States, including the period of the Thirteen Colonies, is about 368,000. Of these, the most notable importers were both Carolinas and Georgia, which together took in more than 200,000 slaves. Other Caribbean colonies, together with French Guiana, reached more than 750,000, bringing the grand total for the 18ᵗʰ-century English slave trade to a whopping 2.38 million, surpassing even the Portuguese. However, it is vital to note that in the same period, the British traders brought more than 2.65 million slaves to the Americas. The difference between the two numbers represents the amount of enslaved people who were sold to other nations, most notably to Spanish Cuba.

When the two centuries of the English slave trade are added up, the grand total of imported human beings reaches slightly more than 2.7 million. That would account for about 27 percent of the total transatlantic slave trade. However, when we add the number of enslaved people the British and American traders transported, it falls just shy of three million people, reaching almost 30 percent of the Atlantic slave trade volume. The British fall only behind the Portuguese when it comes to the numbers. However, a significant difference is that the majority of the English trade was conducted in slightly more than a century. The Portuguese had been pioneers of the slave trade since the late 15th century, while the Brazilians continued to import African slaves until the late 19th century. Thus, it seems likely that had it not been for the moral compassion of some thinkers and politicians, Great Britain would eventually have risen to the top of this infamous hierarchy.

Luckily, the high regard for slavery among the leading European slave nations deteriorated, especially since the number of human beings forcibly transported from Africa to the Americas grew rapidly. Thus, by 1807, England had banned the slave trade, followed by the United States in 1808. However, the transatlantic slave trade persisted throughout the 19th century before it finally died out, ending one of the most disgraceful parts of human history.

Chapter 5 – African Participation

In most cases when talking about the transatlantic slave trade, the focus remains on the European merchants and their role in the trade. While their part was indeed instrumental for the development of the slave trade, the participation of various African tribes and nations shouldn't be overlooked, nor should the effect of the trade on their population and history.

Before delving into how and why the Africans partook in the slave trade, few significant points have to be made. Firstly, the nations spread across the west coast of Africa when the Europeans arrived weren't savage, underdeveloped tribes nearer to prehistoric times than developed civilizations. Any description of such kind is the product of either racism or an attempt to justify the atrocities of the Europeans. A similar thing can be said with how indigenous peoples of the Americas were seen for a long time. In both cases, the European colonists often found nations and cultures that were developed. In the case of Africa, most of the states and societies the Europeans, more precisely the Portuguese, contacted were on a similar level of development as any kingdom on the "Old Continent." They also had developed kingdoms and empires, as we shall see in this chapter. Thus, civilization wasn't ever brought to Africa or to the Americas by the Europeans.

The second notable point to be made is the fact that, culturally speaking, the nations and societies of Africa varied. Too often, they are all mentioned as one, which is suitable from the perspective of simplification. However, it would be wrong to think that the societies of Senegal and Angola, for example, were the same. They may have had some similarities or shared traits, but they also differed in many ways as a result of different historical developments. Additionally, it is important to remember that despite usually being labeled as simply one place, the African continent is huge. Put in perspective, the distance from Senegal to Angola is roughly the length of the European continent, from Spain to the Urals in Russia. In comparison, Africa is three times larger than Europe, and it is the second-largest continent.

Finally, it is worth pointing out that the West African nations and societies weren't secluded from the rest of the world before the arrival of the Portuguese and other European traders and colonizers. There are mentions of trade caravans coming across the Sahara Desert from Roman cities in North Africa. More importantly, numerous African nations had a rather lively trade with the Islamic world. Some Africans even embraced Islam, like, for example, in the Mali or Songhai Empires. These two nations, which dominated the western Sahel, a region between the Sahara to the north and the Sudanian savanna to the south, were firmly a part of the Mediterranean world. The change brought by the arrival of European naval merchants only opened a new trade route for them, though it had the capability for a much wider scope of trade.

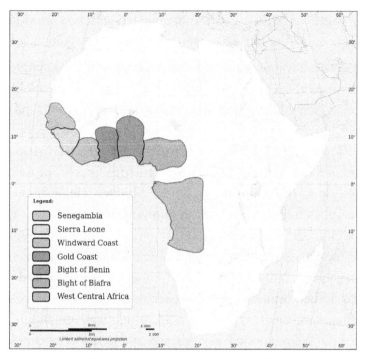

A map of major slave-trading regions in West Africa.
Source: https://commons.wikimedia.org

The Europeans didn't bring the idea of slavery to the West African coast. Various sources and archaeological evidence point to slavery existing in this region since antiquity. However, its scope and form weren't the same throughout the west coast of Africa. For example, most of the smaller nations and tribes from modern-day Senegal to the Ivory Coast usually practiced slavery but on a smaller scale. Most of the enslaved were domestic servants, who often worked alongside their masters. There were even some tribes, like the Efulalu or the Jola in the Senegambia region, that didn't practice slavery at all. In contrast, most of the larger and organized states, like the Songhai and Kongo Empires, practiced slavery on a much larger scale. Another region that practiced slavery more intensely was the Gold Coast, though it wasn't a region occupied by vast states or empires. African regions and states that practiced slavery in a more significant capacity often did so because of trade, as they were all important links in the

African trade network. Thus, they needed a larger workforce to maintain production, but slaves were also traded between nations.

The slave trade was sometimes more localized; for example, some of the Senegambian tribes would sell their slaves to the Gold Coast, where they would be used in mining and other gold producing processes. In other cases, they were exported through what would become known as the Trans-Saharan slave trade. Slaves would be transported from West Africa to North Africa, and from there, they would go on to the Middle East or the Mediterranean. Some of the accounts of such trade date back to antiquity and the ancient Romans and Greeks. By the late medieval period, when the Europeans arrived, the main partners in this trade were the Arabs and other Muslim nations. Nonetheless, the volume of the slave trade at the time was rather limited, and it wasn't a primary economic driving force. That spot was reserved for gold, which was sought after by all civilizations. As mentioned in earlier chapters, the Portuguese were initially interested primarily in the acquisition of that precious metal. In return, they brought dyed clothes and copper ingots and bracelets, all of which the African traders already got from their Muslim trade partners. The main difference was that the Europeans were able to both sell and buy more products since they arrived with large ships.

Despite that, in the early stages of the transatlantic slave trade, the Arab Muslims remained the main trading partner of the coastal African nations. In fact, some modern estimates put them above the Europeans in terms of gold exports throughout this entire period. Here it is vital to remember that slaves weren't seen as the primary trading commodity between the Europeans and Africans until the late 17th and early 18th centuries. This can be illustrated by two facts. One is that until the 1600s, the transatlantic slave trade accounted for only about 25 percent of African slave exports. This changed during the 17th century when the Europeans became the primary exporters of human beings from Africa. Even then, enslaved people still didn't become the most valued export. It was only in the early 18th century that both the volume and overall price pushed the slave trade atop the economic hierarchy in West Africa, topping commodities such as gold, ivory, pepper, and gum. This can be linked with the explosion of sugar production in the Americas and the increasing demand for a workforce.

A major distinction between West Africa and the Americas is the lack of colonization attempts by the Europeans. In the early period of European discoveries, the Portuguese mounted several small-scale attempts to take control of parts of mainland Africa, yet these were largely unsuccessful. They also tried to convert some of the nations since religion was an early motivator, especially in the context of competition with Islam. These were also largely failures. Even when they initially succeeded, like in the case of Kongo, where they enthroned a Christianized ruler in 1506, the local population quickly reverted to their traditional beliefs. The only longer-lasting effect of these attempts was the formation of a mixed-race class of traders, who were an important link between the Europeans and the local populations across the African coast. However, this was not intentional, and while these merchants adopted Christianity and European culture and identified with their European background, they refused to obey the sovereignty of the European states. This mixed-race class was most notable in Afro-Portuguese relations, while the English and French developed these to a much lesser extent.

Regardless, the outright colonization of Africa failed in its initial efforts. The climate and environment proved unsuitable for the Europeans, as malaria and yellow fever wreaked havoc among them. This meant that maintaining a force large enough to preserve control over the conquered lands was too costly. Furthermore, technologies and tactics spread quickly across the African continent, both through European and Arabic contacts. Thus, despite being unable to match European naval supremacy, in the early days of the Atlantic slave trade, African military might was on par with the Europeans. They effectively used both firearms and cavalry, which made it rather difficult for any notable conquests. The Africans also differ much from the indigenous Americans in this regard as well, as the indigenous Americans didn't have enough time to adopt these technologies. Finally, an additional factor was that the African nations overall proved to be quite hostile to any foreign interventions or missionaries. This alone wouldn't be enough, yet the other two major factors helped stave off any significant European colonization efforts for some time.

The end result was that any military gains and conquests were usually short-lived. The best example was the Portuguese attempts in the region of modern-day Angola during the early 16th century. Of course, this didn't stop the Europeans from meddling in local conflicts, yet in general, the nature of Afro-European relations was of peace and respect. The Europeans accepted African religious and political autonomy, at least for the time being. It was only in the 19th century, when the industrialized European nations grew stronger and the impoverished African states became weaker, that colonization was achieved, during which time African societies were remolded. Another thing that European colonization brought to Africa was the abolition of slavery. That fact is rather ironic considering what occurred during the transatlantic slave trade and the role the Europeans had in it.

As has already been mentioned, the slave trade was initially largely voluntary on both sides. A limited volume of people was traded between African and European merchants. This meant that the enslaved people traded to the Europeans could have been attained from traditional sources, whether they were local criminals or captives taken during raids or larger conflicts. Similarly, in those early periods, the Europeans were unable to force local groups or states to partake in the slave trade if they had no wish to do so. The only proactive action the Europeans could do was form trading posts and caravan routes, as well as bring substantial amounts of goods their trading partners desired, creating an economic impetus among the African merchants and rulers. Thus, throughout most of the transatlantic slave trade, there was variation in how and where enslaved people were captured.

Paintings depicting Africans capturing slaves (top) and European and African slave merchants negotiating (bottom). Source: https://commons.wikimedia.org

This fluctuation of the slave trade was caused by numerous economic and political changes in the African states. However, the most notable in these variations were wars. Before the rapid increase in demand for slave labor in the American colonies, most of these intra-African conflicts were caused by preexisting political, economic, or religious struggles. Though the Europeans had their hands in some of them, they rarely caused them. Even their active participation in warfare was occasional at best and limited in scope. Since wars were the largest source of obtaining enslaved people, they also account for much of the sporadic fluctuation in human exports throughout the duration of the Atlantic slave trade, regardless of Europeans' increased or decreased demands for slaves. Some of the best examples can be found in the Gold Coast, which was more of an importer than an exporter of slaves until the 1680s with the escalation of the local Asante wars. Similar developments can be seen in the Senegambia region, which had a burst in exports of enslaved people during the local Islamic religious wars between 1720 and 1740 before returning to its minor role in the slave trade.

However, the Europeans, thanks to their naval-based trade, were able to quickly tap into the ever-changing landscape of the African slave trade. However, it is vital to note that, in some cases, some African nations saw the slave trade as a possible constant source of income. Probably the best example of this is the Kingdom of Kongo. Before the arrival of the Portuguese, this region saw only limited local slavery, yet it quickly organized the slave trade as a way to maintain trade with the Europeans. Its population, led by the elites, developed systemic raiding as a primary source of capturing enslaved people. Due to this, slave exports were the primary branch of Kongo's economy until the 19th century. The steady and constant stream of enslaved humans from the Kingdom of Kongo is also another reason why western-central Africa remained the largest exporting region in the transatlantic slave trade. A similar progression could be seen in the

Kingdom of Dahomey, modern-day Benin, whose economy was also quite centered around the slave trade.

However, there were some African nations that opposed certain aspects of the slave trade. One example would be the Kingdom of Benin, located in present-day Nigeria, not to be confused with modern-day Benin named after the bight. In 1519, the ruling elite banned sales of its own male citizens while also resisting to partake in the large-scale slave trade for a long time. This is surprising since slavery was commonly practiced in the Kingdom of Benin. Their stance changed over time, as the slave trade became the primary economic force in the region, prompting the Kingdom of Benin to finally become an active member of slave exports, though it was done on a much smaller scale than others. This also epitomizes the second characteristic of how the slave trade on the African coast developed. Despite not having the capability to militarily force the slave trade onto African societies, the Europeans used economic pressure to open new markets for the acquisition of enslaved people.

The intentionality of this pressure is debatable. On the one hand, the American demand increased the amount both planters and, in turn, merchants were willing to pay for a single human being. With that, the demand for other African products and resources fell, as traders could earn much more by selling slaves. These processes are universal, though, and are part of economic laws of supply and demand. However, it isn't hard to imagine that particular traders did as much as they could to attain more of this valuable commodity by exerting pressure on their African counterparts. They could have simply given better offers or bribes, threatened them politically or even militarily, or dabbled in local politics. The proof of such practices can be seen in political debates about abolition in early 19th-century Britain. One of the points made was that African nations began waging wars, which were stimulated and encouraged by the Europeans, for the sole purpose of enslaving people. With that, from the mid-18th century onward, large-scale slaving wars became more common among the African nations, replacing the smaller raids of previous centuries.

So far, African participation has been described in a general way, but, as it has been mentioned, there was a lot of variation and different stages of evolution in the slave trade over time. It all started when the Portuguese sailed to the Senegambia region, settling Cape Verde and the banks of the Gambia River. Most of these communities quickly became primarily run by the mixed Afro-Portuguese classes, as high mortality rates plagued the Europeans. While the region was monopolized by the Portuguese, they mainly traded for gold that came from the Bambouk mines located in the Senegambian hinterland. They were also interested in other exotic goods, such as hides from savanna cattle and other local products. The slave trade also quickly rose, as the Portuguese Atlantic domains were in need of a workforce, with the enslaved coming from the coastal Senegambia region and the interior savannas around the Upper Niger River. By the time the Portuguese arrived, the famous Mali Empire had been shattered, leaving several smaller states, most notably Jolof (or Wolof) on the Senegalese coast. In the hinterland, the Songhai Empire began its rise in the mid-15th century, taking most of the Mali territory and its place in trade with the Islamic north.

However, this sole large African empire was toppled by the Moroccans in the 1590s, leaving behind a myriad of smaller states in the hinterland. This proved important for the development of the slave trade, as this ensuing power vacuum among the successor states provided more captives to be sold to the Europeans. By that time, in the late 16th and early 17th centuries, the English and the French had begun trading in the region. The former settled James Island on the Gambia River, while the latter founded Saint-Louis on the Senegal River. By then, the Afro-Portuguese, despite claiming to be solely Portuguese, renounced their supposed motherland's control and traded freely with the Portuguese competitors. On the African side, their most notable trading partner was the Jahaanke (Diakhanke) people from the Upper Niger hinterland. They brought ivory, iron, cotton textiles, kola nuts, and slaves to the coastal regions, mainly using the rivers to navigate. In return, they took various European products, as well as finished textiles and sea salt from the local coastal population.

However, until the 18th century, the enslaved people were just a minor aspect of trade in the region. Since most of them were byproducts of local wars, the supply was unsteady, and the European demand for them was also limited. That changed with the sugar revolution in the late 1600s and even more with the escalation of wars among the Islamic states in the region. These conflicts escalated between 1720 and 1740, as well in the last two decades of the century. These wars were commonly religious wars, or jihads, which were usually led by clerical Fulani tribes and states against more lay-oriented Islamic nations. These wars would then be accompanied by civil wars and other conflicts. Thus, in the 18th century, around 360,000 slaves were exported from the Senegambia region, accounting for roughly 50 percent of its overall participation in the transatlantic slave trade. The commerce of human beings continued into the 19th century, though the volume dropped to less than one-third of the previous century. Overall, roughly 755,000 people were shipped to the Americas from the Senegambia, constituting about 6 percent of the entire Atlantic slave trade.

Farther south from Senegambia is Upper Guinea, a region covering modern-day Guinea-Bissau, Guinea, and Sierra Leone. This was a rainforest area, dotted with even smaller states and, in some cases, even stateless communities. These societies were much less involved in international trade, so they weren't as influenced by Islam. More importantly, it had a less evolved concept of slavery; in some cases, the people didn't even practice it. Local merchants mainly offered kola nuts, beeswax, camwood, ivory, and smaller quantities of gold. The early Portuguese traders were quite interested in these, especially since the slave trade was almost nonexistent. A small change happened during the mid-16th century, though, with the invasion of the Mane people from western Sudan. There was a brief increase in captives for export, but the region still remained largely out of the slave trade network.

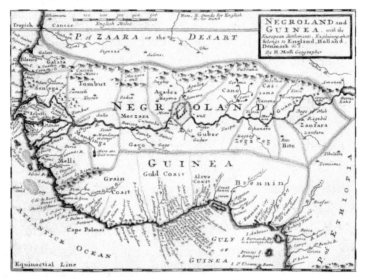

An 18[h]-century map depicting the region from Senegal to Benin.
Source: https://commons.wikimedia.org

Despite first making contact in the mid-15th century, the Portuguese only set up their first trading post in this region in 1588. It was named Cacheu, and it was located at the river of the same name in what is today coastal Guinea-Bissau. They founded Fort Bissau farther south about a century later. By then, the Dutch, the French, and the English had begun trading in the region. The Dutch never managed to maintain the trading fort for a prolonged period, but by the 18th century, the French had established themselves on Gambia Island, while the English settled on Bounce Island, both located in the estuary of the Sierra Leone River. At that time, Upper Guinea became more involved in the slave trade, as numerous captives from the Islamic wars in the hinterland ended up in their hands and were then sold to the Europeans. Thus, the region went from a few thousand exported slaves in the 17th century to over 200,000 throughout the 18th century, with substantial numbers being sold well up to the mid-19th century.

To the southeast of Upper Guinea was a region encompassing modern-day Liberia and the Ivory Coast. Throughout colonial times, this area had various names, like the Windward Coast, Pepper or Grain Coast, and Ivory Coast. The last two names also give a straightforward answer to what the local population, which was divided into several smaller states, exported. What sets this region apart from others is the fact that the coastal region provided few decent landing beaches or harbors, making trade somewhat harder. Because of this, the European presence in this area was limited. In the early 17th century, the Dutch attempted to establish a trading post in what is today Liberia, but it was short-lived. The English returned to the region in the 1660s, mostly looking for pepper. Farther east, in what is today the Ivory Coast, the French established a mission at Assinie in a region bordering the Gold Coast. Yet even with these posts, trade was sparse, especially since by the early 18th century, local elephant herds had been depleted and the Europeans had lost their interest in pepper.

Similar to Upper Guinea, the Windward Coast's participation in the slave trade was minimal throughout most of the transatlantic slave trade until the Islamic wars erupted in the hinterland. During the 18th century, roughly 289,000 slaves were transported to the Windward Coast and sold to the Europeans. By the end of the century, local participation in the slave trade once again returned to the margins. This area had access to such a substantial number of the enslaved because it was better integrated into the interior north-south caravan networks. However, prior to and after this short outburst in the slave trade, the Windward Coast's activity in this field was negligible. Thus, even when combined, Upper Guinea and the Windward Coast sold fewer slaves than the Senegambia. These two regions exported about 724,000 human beings, accounting for less than 6 percent of the total volume of the Atlantic slave trade.

The West African coast spans eastward from the Ivory Coast into the Gold Coast region (modern-day Ghana). In this part of the West African coast, savannas replace the rainforests. When the Portuguese arrived in the 15th century, the region was divided into several smaller nations, which were mainly populated by the Akan people. Even prior to their contact with the Europeans, these states already had quite advanced economies, which were based on gold mining and trade. As such, this region was immediately attractive to the European merchants, as their most sought-after resource at the time was gold. Additionally, the Gold Coast was dotted with suitable harbors and landing beaches. Thus, it wasn't long before the Europeans began building their trading posts here. The first and probably the most notable was Elmina, which was built by the Portuguese in 1482. By the 18th century, there were more than thirty forts in the region, belonging not only to the major slave-trading nations but also to the Swedish, the Danish, and even the Germans.

These forts, unlike most other European trading posts across the West African coast, were properly fortified positions with stone defenses. This was to protect both the precious golden cargo as well as the control over these strategically important locations. It wasn't in vain either, as numerous local wars were fought among the Europeans for control of these locations over the decades. As a result of those, the forts changed hands several times; for example, Elmina was conquered by the Dutch in the 1630s, which the British later took in the late 18th century. Gold remained the primary, if not the only, resource traded in this region until the 1680s. Until that time, there was only the sporadic export of slaves, and during some periods, the Akan people even bought slaves to work in their mines. A series of wars then broke out among the Akan states, leading to the formation of the Ashanti Empire. By the early 18th century, it came to control most of the Gold Coast.

These wars began producing substantial amounts of captives, which the European merchants were glad to buy from the Ashanti. Simultaneously, the production of gold began to drop, probably caused by the wars, adding further economic incentive for the Akan to participate in the slave trade. During the 18th century, some of the Ashanti traders even started buying people from the hinterland, acting as the middlemen in the slave trade with the Europeans. As for the nature of the wars among the Akan people, it seems they were mostly fueled by the struggle for expansion and political dominance. However, some modern scholars think that, especially in the later period, acquiring captives may have become a more crucial motivator. Regardless, as in almost all other regions of the West African coast, the commerce of humans became a primary economic field. Overall, about 1.2 million people were exported from this region, with nearly 90 percent of that being achieved in the 18th century alone. With those numbers, the Gold Coast represents about 10 percent of the total volume of the transatlantic slave trade.

The Gold Coast was also home to one of the earliest regions that adopted American crops. Food crops like maize and manioc were brought over in the early periods of the transatlantic slave trade. Both of these plants were able to revolutionize food production, similarly to the effects of the potato in Europe, as they sustained a much denser population, especially in the later periods. Maize was suitable for the savannas, while manioc played a crucial role in the rainforests, giving more stable forest-agriculture to the region. Other plants were also brought, most notably tobacco, cacao, and peanuts. As the slave trade died out, these plants replaced human beings as one of the African coast's primary exports.

Farther eastward from the Gold Coast was the Bight of Benin. The Slave Coast, as it was also called, extended over modern-day Togo, Benin, and western Nigeria up to the Niger River Delta. The region was dominated by three developed states: the Kingdoms of Dahomey and Benin and the Oyo Empire, the latter of which was located somewhat more in the hinterland. All of these nations were well connected with interior caravan trade routes and a long-lasting tradition of statehood. It was a region of stark contradictions in terms of their approach to the slave trade. While the Kingdom of Benin avoided it until the 18th century, in Dahomey, the slave trade became an important pillar of its economy. The latter was so successful that its port of Ouidah (Whydah) became one of the most important slaving ports on the whole West African coast. It is also important to note that the slave trade was a royal monopoly in the Kingdom of Dahomey at one point.

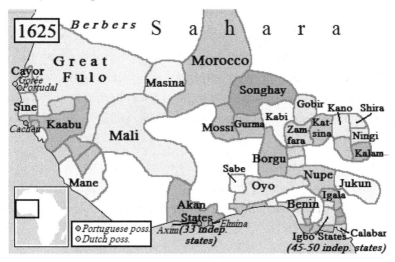

Map of the African states in the early 17th century.
Source: https://commons.wikimedia.org

The Portuguese arrived in the Bight of Benin by the late 15th century, almost immediately beginning trade with the local population. However, at the time, it was small in scope and not oriented toward the slave trade. That changed in the 17th century when the Europeans achieved a more substantial presence in the region, with all major slave-trading nations being active in the area. Despite having their own ports and trading factories, the most notable trading posts remained in the hands of the African states. The Europeans went there, usually respecting the local customs and paying taxes, in order to acquire slaves. Though the main trading good was humans, the Kingdom of Benin, as well as other states in the region, had other resources to export, most notably ivory, palm oil, and pepper.

Dahomey's dominance in the local slave trade was cut short by the Oyo Empire in the 1730s. After a short war, Dahomey became a tributary state, while the Oyo Empire reached the coastline. It also became deeply involved in the slave trade, centering it around the port now known as Porto-Novo. Like in other regions, these more notable conflicts provided for a surge in the supply of enslaved people, as evidenced by increased exports during the Oyo civil wars in the late 18th century. Yet it seems that wars weren't the primary source for slaves. Since they had a steady and prolonged supply of slaves, frontier raids, local judicial and religious practices, and trade with the inner markets must have occurred. Political practices also attributed to it, as there are records of the Oyo Empire demanding slaves as part of the tributes from subjugated polities. The Bight of Benin sold about two million slaves. Just shy of 1.3 million were traded during the 18th century alone. The Bight of Benin continued its participation in the slave trade well into the 19th century, making this region the second-largest supplier of enslaved people.

East of the Niger Delta, and spanning southward as well, is the Bight of Biafra. Today, it is also known as the Bight of Bonny, spanning across modern-day eastern Nigeria, Cameroon, Equatorial Guinea, and Gabon. This region had developed urban settlements and trade networks before the arrival of the Europeans. The local Igbo and Ibibio (Efik) peoples used the rivers, most notably the Niger and Cross rivers, to facilitate trade with the hinterland as well as along the coast. Despite that, their polities remained small, as they were mostly city-states centered around coastal ports. Most notable were Bonny, Old Calabar, and New Calabar. These were the centers of local trade and also played a crucial role in contacts with the Europeans. Like in the Bight of Benin, these major trade centers remained under African control, with Europeans visiting them from their local trading posts.

Despite the Portuguese being the first to arrive, the British played the most active role in the region's trade. Initially, the region traded mostly palm oil products and ivory before transitioning into the slave trade around the mid-17th century. However, it seems that this region's export of enslaved people was based more on peaceful trade than wars. Their merchants, most notably ones from the Igbo tribes, traveled inward to gather slaves to sell to the Europeans. At the height of the slave trade in the 18th century, they exported about 900,000 human beings. About 90 percent of this trade occurred in the three already mentioned ports, with the British accounting for about two-thirds of the region's entire slave trade. Overall, about 1.6 million enslaved people were exported from this region, with slave trade activity going to at least the 1830s. The two bights together accounted for about 28 percent of the entire volume of the transatlantic slave trade.

Continuing southward from the Bight of Biafra comes western-central Africa, which covers the modern-day Democratic Republic of Congo, the Republic of Congo, and Angola. This region was well developed prior to the arrival of the Europeans, with substantial copper-mining industries and trade networks. The entire Congo Basin shared a common culture and a unified market, but it was divided into several large kingdoms. North of the Congo Delta was the Kingdom of Loango, while south of it was the Kingdom of Kongo. In their intermediate hinterland laid the Kingdom of Tio, while farther inward, between the Zambezi River and Tanganyika Lake, were the Kingdom of Luba and the Lunda Empire. Farther south, on what is today the Angolan coast, rose the Kingdom of Ndongo. Both Ndongo and Kongo rose to prominence around the time the Portuguese arrived, with the latter becoming the largest African state below the equator.

Despite the region being dotted with several larger states, as well as smaller ones, the Portuguese founded several trading posts, with the most notable being Luanda, which was created in 1575. More importantly, they got involved in local politics almost as soon as they arrived in the region. Initially, they aided the rising Kingdom of Kongo, assisting its most famous ruler, Afonso I (Mvemba a Nzinga), who, during the early 16th century, greatly expanded its territories. Afonso also adopted Christianity, trying to force it as an official state religion while closely cooperating with the Portuguese and trading ivory, copper, and slaves. He enacted a royal monopoly over the slave trade, though he tried to limit its effects on his people by banning the export of his subjects. Afonso even appealed to both Lisbon and Rome to rein in the Portuguese merchants who began to dabble in the illegal slave trade, destabilizing and depopulating his domain. Of course, his pleas were in vain, as the slave trade only grew.

Around the mid-16th century, the Portuguese redirected their support to the Kingdom of Ndongo, which, prior to that, was in a subjugated position toward Kongo. The Portuguese helped them gain their independence, and in return, they were given permission to form Luanda. By the early 17th century, the Portuguese once again switched their support. They backed the Imbangala mercenaries in forming the Kasanje Kingdom in the hinterland, who were struggling against both Ndongo and Kongo. However, the Portuguese weren't the only ones capable of playing such games. All three kingdoms allied with the Dutch in 1641 when they attempted to seize Portuguese possessions in the region. However, with Brazilian aid, the Portuguese restored their domain in the 1660s. Along the way, they once again allied with Kongo, as they helped them defend their state from invaders from the interior. From then on, the Portuguese remained heavily entrenched in the region, dominating trade with the area south of the Congo River. By the 18th century, they even began expanding to the immediate hinterland. This is the only example of such penetration into the hinterlands on the entire West African coast before the 19th century, as the other countries were limited to trading ports. This region also became the largest center of Afro-Portuguese, who began to take over the slave trade with the locals south of Luanda.

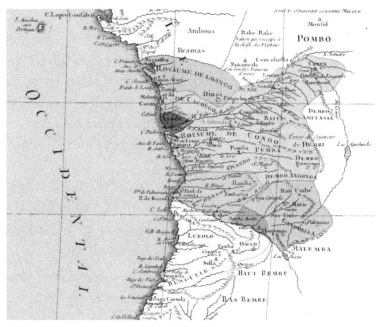

A map of the Congo region in 1770. Source: https://commons.wikimedia.org

Of course, other European nations tried to penetrate western-central Africa, but with little success. Their activities were mostly limited to the Kingdom of Loango. However, the Europeans remained limited to coastal areas. Thanks to the navigability of the Congo River, this meant the African traders from the interior could actually choose whom to sell their captured slaves. Thanks to the constant wars, as well as organized slave raids, western-central Africa proved to be a constant and a substantial slave exporter since the early 16th century. At the height of the slave trade in the 18th century, this region sold about 2.36 million human beings. Due to its strong ties with Brazil, it continued its high-volume trade in the next century, reaching almost another 2 million people. Overall, western-central Africa sold about 5 million people, while some estimates go up to 5.5

million, making it the largest exporter of slaves in the transatlantic slave trade, accounting for at least 40 percent of its total volume.

The southern tip of the African continent didn't play an important role in the slave trade. In the late 18th and early 19th centuries, Madagascar and Mozambique, located on the eastern shores of Africa, finally joined in. They were under Portuguese rule, and in prior centuries, they were part of the gold trade, as well as an important stop for traders going from Asia to Europe. The slave trade here developed only in the mid-18th century, and it was primarily aimed at the European domains in the Indian Ocean. It was only in the early 19th century that more constant shipments of enslaved people from this region started going to the Americas, primarily Brazil. This was caused both by increasing demand, which meant that the time it took to sail to the Americas became profitable enough, as well as political and economic disruptions in the interior caused by wars and drought. By the end, this east African region supplied about 550,000 slaves to the Americas, with about 440,000 in the 19th century alone. It accounted for less than 5 percent of the total transatlantic slave trade.

This chapter, though vastly condensed, exhibits how the slave trade developed on the African coast, both through time and in geographical terms. It also points out the part played by the local peoples as suppliers to the European traders, creating an international and transcontinental slave trade network.

Chapter 6 – The Experience of the Enslaved People

The above background information was needed to paint the picture of how the slave trade developed. However, it is also vital to paint the human tragedy of the transatlantic slave trade. It is important to remember that every number in the horrendous statistics presented above was a living being, one suffering a rather cruel fate.

It is impossible to tell a single story for all the enslaved people, as there were many differences. Some were criminals, religious captives, or indebted servants. Another smaller percentage were people given as tribute between states. However, most of the enslaved were captured during wars or slave raids. In the first case, they could have been prisoners taken after a battle, though it is likely that more of them were enslaved when an army conquered or even just passed through a region. The slave raids were similar to that, but they happened on a much smaller scale. Regardless, it is highly unlikely that most of the captives were combatants, as many perished in battles. However, the majority were indeed adult males who had the capability to participate in future wars. Lessening an enemy's ability to counterattack was a much-desired side effect of the slave trade among the African states.

Once captured, the enslaved people began the first leg of their journey. Most of them were imprisoned or captured in the interior, so the local slave merchants, who were often part of the same nobility that led the wars, transported them toward the coast. This part of the experience varied a lot. Some were carried on large canoes and boats down the major rivers, like the Congo or Senegal. Others were transported via land caravans, maybe on foot or on some kind of cart. Thus, the length of this voyage differed depending on the local geography, place of capture, and existing trade practices. In some cases, it could be a matter of days, while in other cases, it could weeks or even months. The treatment of the enslaved also varied substantially. It is thought that enemies from wars would be treated harsher, with more physical abuse and less food. Nutrition would also depend on the culture's social norms, as well as economic and climate factors. Also, not all merchants took their slaves through the entire journey to the coast. Ones hailing from the far interior most likely sold their enslaved people to other traders along the continental slave trade network, creating a merchant chain to the coast.

Once an enslaved person arrived at a port, they had to wait. Although it might seem like the slave trade never stopped, the departures of slave vessels weren't that common. Furthermore, depending on local bureaucracies and customs, slaves might have had to wait before the European traders finalized their deal, pay their tribute, and get the clearance to board the slaves on their ships. It is also possible that in some cases, the Europeans had to wait for their African partners to gather enough enslaved humans to fill their ships, as it was important to maximize their gain. Once again, the treatment of the enslaved people while they waited depended on numerous local conditions, with the most notable being political and ecological stability. If there were no major wars, political upheavals, or droughts, the waiting period was much more tolerable. If nothing else, the captives would be fed enough, as their lives meant more profit. In contrast, if there were food shortages, they were the last to be fed.

Furthermore, geographical location also played a role, as certain regions were more prone to various diseases like malaria or yellow fever.

Two illustrations depicting slave trade caravans in Africa.
Source: https://commons.wikimedia.org

Regardless of these circumstances, it is certain that the enslaved people suffered while they waited. Any favorable treatment was more an exception than the rule, and many of the captives had no clue what was to be their fate. The extent of this physical and psychological torment can only be imagined. Overall, modern scholars estimate that, on average, an enslaved person waited between six to twelve months before being loaded on a ship. During this time, which includes being transported to the coast, many of the enslaved perished, whether from starvation, from disease, or from the maltreatment and cruelty of their captors. The numbers are hard to evaluate, especially when it comes to their transportation to the coast, as there are almost no written records of this. However, since the enslaved people were taken along already established trade routes, with more or less developed slavery systems, it is unlikely the number of deaths was extraordinarily high. Also, not all captives were destined for the Atlantic trade, as some were sold along the way to locals.

For the deaths on the coast, some estimations can be made by evaluating European records. Of more than fifty Dutch voyages made in the late 17th and early 18th centuries, roughly 5 percent of purchased slaves died before they even left the continent. However, it is likely that this figure varied considering the number of variables that impacted the mortality rate among the enslaved. Yet it was only the beginning of their suffering, as they then would be boarded on ships, going on yet another long journey. Here it is important to address one of the most widely talked about aspects of the transatlantic slave trade: the overcrowding of ships. An image of African slaves piled up like sardines is something that has been widely accepted as an iconography of what has become known as the Middle Passage. Those conditions were heralded as the cruelest aspect of the slave trade and blamed as the cause for the high mortality rate of the transported enslaved people.

However, recent studies have shown that these were largely exaggerations made by the abolitionists when they fought to end the slave trade. Modern scholars have examined various ship sizes from different nations and throughout much of the transatlantic slave trade's duration. They believe that between five and six square feet were allotted per enslaved person on average. This number rose to between seven and eight square feet in the late 18th and early 19th centuries. Those are abysmally small spaces for a single person to occupy. A simple comparison would be to a modern prison, which usually mandates about forty square feet per inmate. There is no doubt that the enslaved people were packed to the brim. But while these conditions are inhumane, scholars have rejected the idea that overcrowding was the primary cause of the high mortality rate on the Middle Passage.

This can be seen in the fact that early slave voyages marked an average mortality rate of 20 percent or higher. Over time, this percentage dropped to around 10 percent or less. An example of this drop can be made by examining the British slave trade. A parliamentary committee reported the losses of about 23 percent in the 1680s. This number dropped to around 9 percent between 1761 to 1791, with the percentage dropping to about 4 percent in the last decade of the slave trade. However, it should be noted that by then, the British were below the international average. Nonetheless, a marginal increase in space allotted per captive wouldn't have accounted for such a dramatic drop in the mortality rate.

When comparing mortality rates, modern researchers found that the area from where the ship set sail played a substantial factor. The voyages originating from the northern regions, down to the Gambia River, as well as the southernmost regions in Congo and Angola, had a notably lesser mortality rate than those that hailed from closer to the equator. For example, including journeys from the early 17th century, ships from western-central Africa had on average a mortality rate of about 9.5 percent, while ones from the Bight of Biafra had around

17.4 percent. This can be explained by the fact that in the jungle and tropical regions of the Gold Coast and the two bights, the people were more susceptible to deadly diseases like malaria or yellow fever. Thus, the enslaved would bring these diseases with them on board, which, in the tightly packed decks, would lead to high death rates. In this aspect, overcrowding did indirectly lead to more deaths.

Other local factors played a role as well. Sporadic socioeconomic disturbances, which often coincided with a higher export of human beings, created the circumstances for less food and harsher treatments of the enslaved people while still on the African continent. This would, in turn, weaken their overall health, making it less likely they would survive the transatlantic voyage. Furthermore, some scholars point out that in such times of crisis, the African merchants sold more women and children, who were less likely to endure such horrific conditions. However, fit male captives remained the most desired for the planters in the Americas and were the most trafficked.

Another significant factor was the length of a journey. The shorter the voyage, the fewer people would die. This may actually be one of the most important factors that led to a lesser mortality rate, as over the centuries, the travel time between continents shortened from about three months to roughly six weeks. In extreme situations, the trip could be as short as a single month, but it could also go up to nearly half a year. The length of the journey varied on sailing technologies, the crew's capability, and the luck with winds, as well as the starting and ending points. For example, sailing from Angola to Brazil was much shorter than sailing farther north to the Caribbean or the North American mainland. On the shorter voyages, there was less time for fatal outcomes of diseases or weakened health from terrible living conditions. In contrast, any unplanned prolongation of travel time would lead to the shortage of food, causing starvation and more death.

Here it is worth noting that the European sailors suffered from similar issues. Diseases would often spread among the crew as well, and food shortages affected everyone on board. Thus, the death rates among the sailors also went up to 20 percent on average in the early days, dropping in the later centuries of the transatlantic slave trade. This offers additional proof that overcrowding was only a contributing factor to the high death rate, as crews were affected as well, even though they had slightly better living conditions on board.

Regardless, the treatment of the enslaved people was beyond cruel. Firstly, they were taken into small holdings before heading on to the open seas without any idea where they were going. They were surrounded by strangers who often spoke a different language. The holdings below the deck were often smelly, with stale air and low light. The men were usually chained to prevent mutinies, as the crew was heavily outnumbered by the enslaved people. The women and children were sometimes left unbound as they were seen as less of a threat. All of this caused severe trauma among the enslaved people, which was noted by contemporaries. Melancholy, depression, and other psychological disorders were common. This, in turn, led to a loss of appetite, dehydration, servility, and in some cases suicide, as some of the captives saw their circumstances as a punishment worse than death.

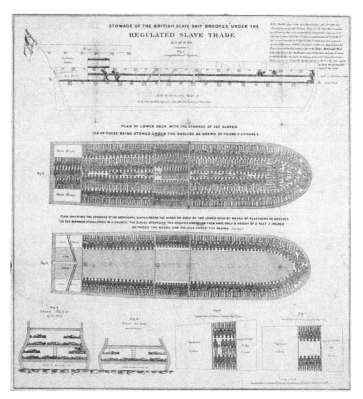

Diagram showing a late 18ᵗʰ-century British slave ship after the new regulations were imposed. Source: https://commons.wikimedia.org

As already stated, the enslaved people suffered from various diseases. Besides tropical illnesses, such as malaria, dysentery, also known as the flux at the time, was also quite common. Poor hygiene contributed to its presence, and the lack of any proper medicine meant it was deadly. If it was possible, those with the flux were isolated, but that wasn't always the case. Scurvy, which is caused by a lack of vitamin C, plagued both the crew and the enslaved people. However, by the mid-18ᵗʰ century, this was recognized, and ships began treating it with doses of lemons or oranges, lowering its deadliness. In cases of smallpox, primitive inoculations were sometimes practiced, though more often, the crew tried to separate the diseased from the healthy. As for malaria, by the mid-17ᵗʰ century, chewing cinchona tree bark became a somewhat accepted treatment.

However, the availability of all these medicines and knowledge varied from ship to ship, as well as the crew's will to take care of the enslaved people.

Even though there was a lack of humanity among the slave traders, their lust for profits was strong. As the prices of the slaves rose, the traders realized it was worth putting more effort into saving their lives. Thus, from the late 17th to the early 18th century, changes began to affect the slave trading industry. Ships began employing doctors of various qualities and capabilities while also arming the sailors with medical handbooks if surgeons were deemed too costly. This shouldn't be taken as anything more than just basic healthcare, as it simply became apparent that better hygiene and fresh air would fetch them even more profit. If the weather allowed it, some of the enslaved people were brought up on the deck, in some cases even forced to exercise through dance or other activities. This helped their physical and, to a smaller degree, psychological condition. Additionally, in the later periods when ships were being built with the slave trade in mind, the space below the deck was streamlined and fitted with ventilation openings to allow a steady flow of fresh air.

The governments played only a minor role in bettering the enslaved people's treatment in the Middle Passage. The Portuguese passed a law concerning the number of slaves allowed according to a ship's size while also mandating enough supplies be brought on board for a voyage of an average length. These were only minimal restrictions. No other nation passed any similar laws until 1788 when Britain also regulated the number of enslaved people per carrying ton, as well as a mandatory ship doctor. However, these laws made no provisions on the mistreatment of the enslaved people. This was left up to the will of the crew, which was often more torturous than not. The European sailors used harsh physical punishments to assert control over the able-bodied captives who substantially outnumbered them. Beatings and whippings were the most common forms of punishment; however, crueler ones would be used if a rebellion was attempted. In those cases, captains often chose not only to kill the rebels but also to instill fear in others to prevent it from happening again. Various forms of torture were used in those cases, which would eventually lead to painful deaths. The frequency of insurrections is debated. One modern study estimates that they occurred on less than 2 percent of voyages, while another one pushes that number up to 10 percent. However, they were rarely successful. Regardless, most captains tried to avoid both overly cruel punishments and rebellions before they began, as they cut into profits.

Under normal conditions, the enslaved people would be fed two times a day, usually beans or rice. Other common foods were corn and yams, along with other various vegetables. Citrus fruits were also occasionally added, especially in the later periods, to prevent scurvy. There was little taste in these foods and even less dignity in eating. Ten or more slaves would be placed around a tub containing food, scraping it with wooden spoons. As for drinks, they couldn't expect anything more than water. When the enslaved people refused to eat or drink, the crew would try to force them, as they knew it was crucial for better profits. However, in cases when there was a shortage, such "humanity" would cease. One of the most infamous examples happened in 1781 on a British ship named the *Zong*, which run out of fresh water, prompting its captain to throw more than a hundred bound Africans overboard, hoping the insurance would cover their supposed natural deaths.

There seems to be little reason behind why the slave traders tried to strip their captives of their identities and culture. It was more than likely a byproduct of trying to keep the enslaved people in order, especially if they came from a region the Europeans saw as more rebellious. In most cases, it seems the captive Africans maintained their base culture, language, and identity. The damage was more likely on a more personal level, as the traumas they survived would often scar them for life. However, the shared suffering in the bowels of the ship created a new kind of identity for the slaves; despite the language barriers between the various groups, they shared similar cruel fates. Such comradery often lasted for years after the voyage.

Finally, after weeks or months of travel, the ships would reach the Americas. Of course, their suffering wasn't over. The ships would first wait in the harbors, and then the enslaved people would be kept in confinement, waiting to be sold to their new masters. More of them perished as they waited. Some of the captives were employed where they had arrived or at least nearby. In some cases, a new journey awaited them, as they were either reshipped to other parts of the Americas, most notably if they were destined to go to the Spanish mainland, or to the Brazilian interior. These journeys provided additional peril for the enslaved people. Eventually, one way or another, the slaves would reach their final destination, where they would spend the rest of their days working.

The enslaved people engaged in a wide variety of work. Only a marginal minority went to the urban centers to act as personal servants of some sort. Most were sent to plantations, working on producing sugar, tobacco, cotton, and coffee. A considerable number also went to work in the mines. Even when singling a specific field, like, for example, sugar production, the harshness of a slave's life and their work are hard to generalize. It depended on the region, time period, type of skill one possessed, the local colonial slaving rules, and even the master's personality. In some cases, these conditions were more bearable, while in others, they were beyond inhumane, pushing the enslaved people literally to death.

Illustration of 19th-century slaves in Brazil.
Source: https://commons.wikimedia.org

Overall, the enslaved people were treated as property, not as human beings. This is especially evident in the various slave codes passed throughout this time. They usually weren't allowed to legally marry, have any kind of possessions, or assert any control over their lives. The enslaved people had to do what they were told, as any act of disobedience, or even worse rebellion, was severely punished with beatings or lashings. Attempts to run away or revolt were punishable by death in most cases. All of this was done to instill servility among the enslaved population, as they usually outnumbered their white masters, just as on the ships. Their cruel treatment didn't end there. As with any property, some white masters thought they could do with their slaves as they pleased, regressing to various forms of torture while also raping enslaved women. This is evidenced by the emerging mixed-race class, as well as by certain laws that prohibited the offspring of a white master and black slave from inheriting their father's property and titles, which was the tradition among all European nations.

There was also a form of cultural suppression, as the planters often attempted to instill their own culture, tradition, and beliefs, replacing the customs and faiths the enslaved had brought from Africa. This could begin as early as on the African shores, where some of them were initially baptized. However, this was often done as moral absolution, be it in front of the church or for one's own beliefs, as it represented "civilizing" the Africans. There was often a law that demanded the enslaved people be baptized before entering service in the colonies, so, in some cases, this was done in the Americas as well. But since most slaves were forced into this, they had no real interest nor any actual understanding of the Christian tradition. For this reason, their masters often tried to forcibly replace their African identities with European traditions. To achieve that, they used various physical and psychological punishments, especially if the owner was a zealot.

Depiction of flogging, a common punishment of the enslaved people throughout the Americas. Source: https://commons.wikimedia.org

In return for their work, the enslaved people received barely anything. In some cases, laws demanded they had to be fed and given basic clothes or even shelter. Additionally, by providing for the basic needs of the enslaved people, they could focus more on their work while reducing their communal ties, making them dependent on their masters. Yet, in some cases, the masters left the enslaved people to fend for themselves, from growing their own food to erecting a shelter. This made their lives even harder, but it made them more self-sufficient and allowed for the formation of families, their own localized community, and culture. It is important to note that another problem when it came to creating families was the imbalance between the sexes. According to modern estimates, women, on average, made up only about one-third of the imported slaves, with some regions having even worse ratios. This meant that regardless of other circumstances, a substantial number of enslaved men simply couldn't find a partner.

This led to another problem, at least from a demographic perspective. The slave population had a rough time reproducing, notwithstanding the fact that it is likely many didn't want to bring up children in the living hell they endured. This partly explains why the slave population didn't grow quickly, even though it might seem that way with the millions of Africans being brought to the Americas. Another terrifying fact contributing to this was the high mortality rate among the enslaved people. According to a modern study, at some points, the average survival rate in the first two or three years was only 50 percent. However, it seems the rate of about one in three deaths in the period of so-called "acclimatization" was a more general average, with it dropping to "only" 25 percent in the late 18th century. The most common reasons for death were diseases and harsh labor. To paint a larger picture of this tragedy, about 2.3 million enslaved people arrived in the British Caribbean islands from the 17th to the early 19th century. However, at the eve of abolition, there were only roughly 775,000 slaves in these colonies. It should be pointed out that this roughly 33 percent survival rate disregards the deaths on the Middle Passage, as well as the fact that a minor number of the living slaves were children of earlier generations.

Overall, the traumas and personal suffering that each of the enslaved human beings went through are hard to generalize and encompass in a short chapter. Furthermore, using percentages and large number adds to their dehumanization, yet it is necessary to understand what they went through, especially the magnitude of it all. It shouldn't be forgotten that some of the worst sides of humanity were exhibited during the transatlantic slave trade and, even more importantly, that innocent people suffered because of that.

Chapter 7 – The Slow Death and the Effects of the Slave Trade

The growth and expansion of the transatlantic slave trade was a long and slow process, guided more by laws of the economy than by purposeful design. In contrast, its end was orchestrated by people focused on such a goal, aiming to do it quickly. Unfortunately, for many Africans, that end didn't come fast enough.

During the 18th century, the slave trade was going through its "golden" age in terms of volume and profits. It rose from the sidelines of the global slave trade into one of its most vital branches. With that came important changes to how it was conducted. Since the late 17th century, but even more prominently in the 18th century, slave merchants began crafting specialized slaving vessels. They were built to maximize gains by providing the enslaved with more chances for survival. This included the already mentioned better ventilation but also copper plating and a decrease in the ship's size, both of which made travel quicker. This also led to a decrease in the triangularity of the transatlantic slave trade, a feature that is often emphasized. This meant that a single ship would carry goods from a European port to Africa in exchange for enslaved people. Then it would travel to the

Americas and exchange the slaves in return for spices and other valuable products and finally go back to Europe.

However, as the 18th century passed, the smaller slaving ships often disregarded taking much of the valuable American produce. Sometimes the slavers didn't even bother taking any of it at all, especially when prices of, for example, sugar dropped, as their gains wouldn't be as high. They chose currency or precious metals instead. With this increase in volume and overall prominence also came the increase in notoriety. The transatlantic slave trade started generating serious opposition, which slowly grew in size and willingness to fight what they viewed as a despicable act unbecoming of human beings.

These new sentiments could be traced to the ideals of the Age of Enlightenment, an intellectual movement that began to reshape European thought in the 17th century. Many of the famous thinkers of that period, like John Locke or Jean-Jacques Rousseau, believed in the natural rights of humans, which weren't linked to any laws or customs. One of these chief rights was, of course, freedom. Such ideas inspired the American and the French Revolutions, but they also swayed many people to consider slavery as something inhumane. Thus, many prominent intellectuals began to voice their opposition to slavery and the slave trade. They often believed that stopping the slave trade would eventually lead to the complete abolition of slavery. It was a valid assumption, though it took slightly longer than they expected. These secular ideas seeped over into religion as well, most notably among the Quakers and the Protestant Evangelicals.

Prior to that, the Old Testament was used to justify slavery, as it referenced it without any negative sentiments. However, with the ideals of natural rights and an overall focus on humanist morality coming to the forefront, some religious groups began interpreting the Bible differently, focusing on the idea of "good will towards all men." This understanding of the holy texts rendered slavery as something completely against Christian ideals. In fact, while the Enlightenment thinkers were still entrenched in philosophical debates over the issue of slavery, the Quakers were actively working toward the abolition of slavery and the slave trade. They wrote petitions and voiced their concerns in the last years of the 17th century, and by the mid-1700s, they began imposing rules that banned Quaker ties with any slave activities. By the late 18th century, they began forming anti-slavery societies both in the US and England, asking their governments to ban the slave trade. These groups became the primary driving force behind the legal end of the British and US slave trade in 1807.

British abolitionist badge pleading for the humanity of the enslaved people. Source: https://commons.wikimedia.org

Enlightenment ideas also spilled over into the economy. Coinciding with this was the emergence of modern capitalism. One of the chief ideals of this economic system was paid labor. Slavery went against these sentiments, so a serious opposition to slavery formed in the rising middle class. However, this was only partially motivated by moral or philosophical beliefs. Small business owners and industrialists, rising in the economic hierarchy, didn't employ slave labor for many other reasons. Chief among them was the fact that their enterprises needed a skilled workforce and that they were located in societies that weren't based on forced labor anymore. As such, they saw slavery as unfair for economic competition. Banning it would also improve their gains, and they also hoped that ending the slave trade would make Africa a more stable market to export finished goods and import raw materials like oil or metals. Animosity toward slavery could also be found in the political competitions between the old high class, whose wealth was at least partially based on forced servitude, and the new industrial high class. The latter was hoping to gain the upper hand by cutting off one source of the former's profits.

Apart from that, many scholars have claimed that by the late 18th century, the slave trade and the sugar plantations were generating less profit than before, prompting yet another reason why it was banned in the early 19th century. However, some modern researchers reject these ideas. Their studies show that the British West Indies were still generating substantial profit when the slave trade was abolished, while the southern US states were still mainly financed by their cotton exports. Even after the abolition of the slave trade, and even of slavery in general, British sugar was still competitive in the global market. However, it is important to note that the technological advances of the Industrial Revolution created a lesser need for labor, as at least some processes in both the sugar and cotton industries were mechanized and powered by steam or other types of energy. For example, the first steam-powered sugar mill was installed in Jamaica in 1768. Nonetheless, at the time, these technological novelties were not advanced enough to replace the majority of the human labor, so the use of slaves could still be profitable and useful.

Another important factor in the push toward abolitionism was the activity of the liberated slaves. Many of the Africans who managed to attain freedom used their experiences to advocate for the ban of slavery, exposing how cruel it was through their own personal stories. Examples of this would be the works of Olaudah Equiano and Ottobah Cugoano in Britain, as well as Jeanne Odo and Jean-Baptiste Belley in France. They provided voices for the hundreds of thousands of voiceless slaves in the Americas. Their activities provided ammunition for abolitionist propaganda, yet it seems that the success of revolt on Saint Domingue played a more crucial role. It proved that if pushed to the brink, the enslaved people could effectively fight back. This prompted some of the politicians, at least those without any direct link to slavery or the slave trade, to opt for the ban as a way to protect the colonies from serious rebellions and maintain European rule over them. Thus, the enslaved, in one way or another, contributed to the end of slavery.

In the end, it is hard to determine which of these factors was the chief reason behind the abolition of the slave trade and, in turn, slavery in general. It was clearly an amalgamation of rising humanist ideals that spread compassion for one's fellow man mixed with economic and political motivations. However, it is important to note that abolition came to fruition only after the idea became profitable, not only in a strictly economic way, to a fraction of powerful people, whose reasons were far from altruistic.

Regardless, as the transatlantic slave trade was reaching its pinnacle at the turn of the 18th century, the abolitionist movements began achieving initial success. Here it is significant to mention that their fight against the slave trade was ultimately aimed at slavery in general, yet this part of the slave chain was the weakest link. Merchants had less political power and were less influential, while the Middle Passage proved to be an easier propaganda target, with the enslaved people cooped up in the dark and foul space below the deck. In contrast, owners of plantations often had stronger political ties and were generally part of the older aristocratic families, and the work in the fields was much harder to present to the general public as something shocking or inhumane. As a result, certain US colonies and later independent states began passing laws that limited the slave trade and, in some cases, even slavery. The anti-slave trade associations also managed to press the British Parliament to pass laws regulating the slave trade. By then, it had become apparent that England was moving toward banning the slave trade in general, as the idea was gaining popularity among the wider public.

Anticipating such a change to occur, the Danish became the first European nation to pass a law banning the slave trade in 1792 though it wouldn't come into effect until 1803. As a lesser slave-trading nation, their exiting the slave stage wasn't as influential. Then came the abolition of slavery in revolutionary France in 1795, though it was short-lived, as Napoleon restored it in 1802. In 1807, Britain finally banned the slave trade, including both on British soil as well as most of its foreign partners. The United States followed suit, banning the import of slaves in early 1807, although the law didn't come into effect until 1808. This was the turning point in the transatlantic slave trade. Not only were two important slave-trading nations opting out of this economic atrocity, but the English were bent on forcing such ideas on all other countries.

However, the slave trade was far from over. Most other nations were still interested in continuing the commerce of human beings, most notably Spain, as Cuba was just beginning to develop sugar production. Even the United States was still active in the slave trade, supplying the Spanish despite banning the import of enslaved people. The British tried to use its maritime superiority to enforce its new anti-slave trade position. In 1808, the Royal Navy formed the West African Squadron, which was tasked with enacting a slave trade blockade, searching any suspicious vessels, and seizing them if any slaving activity was found. Furthermore, the British pressured other slave-trading nations, like Portugal, Sweden, and the Netherlands, to sign treaties restricting the commerce of human beings in the early 1810s. By 1815, after the final defeat of Napoleon's France, Britain imposed the overall condemnation of the slave trade in the Congress of Vienna, securing at least vocal support in the matter from all major European nations and the United States. At the same time, France also abolished the slave trade.

Although it seems as if the slave trade was all but finished by then, ending it proved to be a much more daunting task. Some of the nations seldom enforced abolition, while illicit merchants from all nations started to satisfy the American markets' demand. The British reacted by signing several bilateral treaties with some of the nations, like Portugal and Spain, confirming the end of the slave trade along with gaining the legal right to search ships under their flag. Of course, this caused much friction between the nations, as many saw it as Britain trying to protect its slave-free production in the Caribbean against the supposedly superior forced labor of other nations. Yet the idea of abolition started to internalize in those societies as well. The mainland Portuguese, for example, had been retreating from the slave trade for a while, with the business being handed over to the Brazilians instead, who won independence in 1822. Around this same time, other South American colonies fought for their freedom, slowly joining in the struggle against both the slave trade and slavery in general.

Illustration of slaves being liberated in the Sierra Leone region.
Source: https://commons.wikimedia.org

Over the decades, all the nations accepted the ban of the slave trade, with Brazil being among the last major participants to officially do so in 1831. However, the illegal trade continued to flourish. Locally, some of the national navies intercepted the illicit traders, freeing the captured slaves back on African shores, though not necessarily to the region they were originally from. The Sierra Leone region was one of the most notable places this occurred. The illegal trade also brought the mortality rates back up, along with the cruel handling of the enslaved people. The merchants were now forced to hide, acting more like pirates than traders. Between 1808 and 1860, the British navy seized about 1,600 ships, freeing roughly 150,000 people. Yet this was just a fraction, as roughly three million enslaved people were shipped between 1810 and 1866. By the early 1870s, the slave trade was pretty much dead, as all the major slave-trading nations not only banned the trading of people but also began to actively fight against it. The last important turnaround was the US Civil War, which saw the end of America's participation in slavery.

By then, modern scholars estimate about 12.5 million enslaved Africans had been sent to the Americas. Yet only about 10.7 million arrived. Here it is important to note that the numbers vary, going from as low as 9.5 million to as high as 17 million. The discrepancies in those estimates come from the question of counting embarks or disembarks, adding or disregarding the approximations of people dying in Africa on their way to the slave ports, adding or ignoring the estimations of illicit trades, and other variables. However, the range between 10 and 12 million is an average most scholars agree upon. Regardless of what number is accepted as closest to the truth, it is undeniably a huge number of people who endured through some of the vilest fates imaginable. People were ripped out of their homelands, transported across half of the world in despicable conditions, with many succumbing to various diseases and torture before being worked to death by their new masters.

There were other impactful side effects that go beyond the personal trauma of every single human being that suffered from the transatlantic slave trade. The two that probably first come to mind are economic and demographic influences, yet those are highly debated among scholars due to the rather complex nature of the slave trade across the Atlantic. Some claim that the combined surplus of profits from the slave trade and sugar production by the slave workforce enabled an influx of capital that at least helped the industrialization of Europe, most notably England, which was the first industrial nation in the world. This rapid economic growth and development of new technologies, which allowed such advances, coincided with Britain's participation in the slave trade, yet there are few direct links. Additionally, according to some estimates, the sugar and slave industries generated only between 1 and 5 percent of the total British economy. Regardless, though the slave trade likely wasn't instrumental in kickstarting the Industrial Revolution, it is possible it provided some early surplus to invest in the development of new technologies.

Similar arguments have been made in regard to the African economy. One side argues that the slave trade infringed on it. At the start of the slave trade between the two continents, both Europe and Africa exported or imported both raw goods and finished products. Yet, as the slave trade developed in volume, the Europeans began taking mostly the enslaved while exporting their produced goods, thus, in effect, stifling local industrial capabilities. It is important to note that the Europeans exported weapons and other military products, which affected the African states in their internal conflicts. However, since the trade was largely willing on the African side as well, it is easy to assume that the local elites at least saw gains in dealing with the Europeans. Furthermore, through this trade, some of the important food crops were imported, though this would become more significant in later periods when Africans needed to sustain a much larger population.

This leads to the question of demographic impact on West Africa. What is undeniable is that Sub-Saharan Africa at best stagnated in its population over the duration of the transatlantic slave trade, remaining at around 100 million or slightly less. Yet during the same period, its share in the overall world population dropped from about 18 percent in the 16th century to just about 6 percent in 1900. However, scholars disagree on what caused this. Some have argued it was directly linked to the Atlantic slave trade, but this seems unlikely, as over the same period, but more prominently in the 19th century, around fifty million Europeans migrated willingly to the Americas, yet Europe's population grew. The more plausible cause was the imbalance between genders. In many West African areas, females began outnumbering males, who were chiefly exported to the Americas, making copulation much harder. On top of that, the economic disruption of traditional industries also caused disturbances in population growth, as less material production meant fewer people could be sustained. Some scholars have also stipulated that due to the different nature of their economy, as compared to Europe, the population loss caused by the African slave trade was sufficient enough to cause a demographic and economic demise. Possible proof of this is that its population quickly grew when the slave trade ended, even prior to any significant medical or technological advances arriving in the region.

A less debatable consequence of the Atlantic slave trade was the formation of a new unique Afro-American population and culture in the Americas. The tightly concentrated slave populations created their own traditions and customs, an amalgamation of their African roots, harsh slave life, and the European influences imposed by their masters. This proved to be important in the development of the young American nations in the 19th century, especially when the formerly enslaved people were the majority. One of the best examples of this would be blues music, which is now a worldwide phenomenon. However, it began its life among the slaves in the cotton fields in the southern US. Other influences can be found in cuisine, clothing, language, and beyond. However, with that came the legacy of racism, which follows the Afro-Americans to this day.

The transatlantic slave trade wasn't born out of racism. Yet after centuries of subjugation, forced labor, and various justifications, explanations, or rationalizations, racism undeniably developed as a consequence of the slave trade. Its reach was not limited only to the Americas, as it seeped over to Europe as well. It began as cultural racism, which saw the Africans as lesser barbarians and uncivilized humans. However, by the 19th century, some people believed the Africans were genetically inferior and lesser human beings. This partly explains why some European masters had no trouble being so cruel toward the enslaved people. Unfortunately, this particular negative legacy of the Atlantic slave trade proved to be rather hard to suppress, as racism remains one of the troubles of the modern world.

Beyond this, there were many other effects and impacts of the transatlantic slave trade, though they were less important in the grand scheme of things. Yet all of those seem to pale in comparison to the suffering and death imposed upon the enslaved African people, who were victims of greed and prejudice. For this reason, the end of the Atlantic slave trade couldn't have come soon enough.

Epilogue

The end of the slave trade prompted several crucial changes, most notably the abolition of slavery. Like many societies that argued against the transatlantic slave trade had predicted, ending the trade of humans allowed for the gradual end of institutionalized slavery. Following the precedent set by independent Haiti, other former colonies in Latin America also banned slavery after they gained their freedom. By 1833, England had banned it as well, prompting other nations to follow. For example, France abolished it in 1848, the US in 1865, and Portugal in 1869. Many others did the same around the same time, with Brazil being the last major Atlantic slave-trading and slave-owning nation to ban it in 1888.

A painting depicting the celebration of the enslaved people upon abolition in the French colonies, 1848. Source: https://commons.wikimedia.org

By then, abolition had become detached from the transatlantic slave trade, as it expanded to encompass the whole world. It became an issue almost all nations found common ground on. As such, numerous international conferences and gatherings were held as the nations tried to put an end to the despicable institution of slavery. Among the earliest examples was the Brussel Conference of 1890, where several major nations gathered in an attempt to formulate an act that would help fight the slave trade in the Kingdom of Kongo, the Ottoman Empire, the East African coast, and the Indian Ocean. Similar humanistic ideals continued to pervade society as abolition continued to spread across the globe in the 20th century. This proved to be one of the cornerstones of the League of Nations, which was formed after World War I and was the precursor to the United Nations. The UN, which aims to maintain peace, security, and friendly relations among the nations, declared slavery as being opposed to basic human rights in 1948.

Since then, almost every country around the world has abolished slavery and, with it, the slave trade. There is almost no one who still publicly argues for it, as it is generally condemned as vile and inhumane. Despite that, slavery is very much alive. According to various researchers and organizations, there are between twelve and thirty million slaves around the world today. Virtually none of them are chattel slaves like the ones in the transatlantic slave trade. Most of them are bonded or indebted laborers, as well as coerced workers. Also, a considerable number of them are trafficked humans, including victims of sex trafficking. As such, the global struggle against slavery is still a cause that deserves our focus and support.

Conclusion

The transatlantic slave trade represents a dark and shameful part of human history, one that instills disgust and anger among many to this day. Even worse, unlike many other historical occurrences, it doesn't have a singular culprit or instigator. It is not something that can be blamed on someone. It is a part of our shared historical guilt as humanity, and it is something that shouldn't be avoided. This can be even more infuriating for some, as there are no easy ways to explain why it came to be or why it lasted so long. Even so, the Atlantic slave trade was one of the seminal points in world history, as its influence spanned across continents, centuries, and civilizations. It changed our economy, culture, morals, and more. It shaped how our shared story developed, for better or for worse. And at the same time, it was undeniably atrocious.

Because of this, it is important to study it, talk about it, and keep it in the spotlight. It is something that, despite the shame or disgust it causes, has to remain in our conscience as a warning to how low humans can go in the "right" conditions. It is something that looms from the shadows even today, as slavery remains an international issue still to be solved. Furthermore, such awful acts left scars among us, from anger to racism, problems that can't be solved without communication and discussion. The first step in that direction is being informed about the slave trade and all its aspects. This guide provides an introduction to it. Hopefully, it gave you a basic idea of the history of the transatlantic slave trade. However, this is just the surface of it. There is so much more to learn about it, even though it is a hard subject. It should also provide an initial push toward coming to terms with the wrongdoing of our past, allowing history to heal our deep societal wounds.

Here's another book by Captivating History that you might like

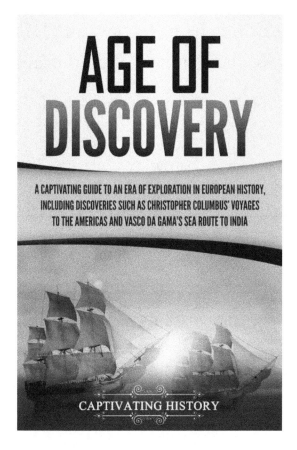

Free Bonus from Captivating History (Available for a Limited time)

Hi History Lovers!

Now you have a chance to join our exclusive history list so you can get your first history ebook for free as well as discounts and a potential to get more history books for free! Simply visit the link below to join.

Captivatinghistory.com/ebook

Also, make sure to follow us on Facebook, Twitter and Youtube by searching for Captivating History.

Bibliography

Anne C. Bailey, *African voices of the Atlantic Slave Trade: Beyond the Silence and the Shame,* Boston, Beacon Press, 2005.

David Eltis and David Richardson, *Extending the Frontiers: Essays on the New Transatlantic Slave Trade Database,* New Haven, Yale University Press, 2008.

David Eltis and David Richardson, *Routes to Slavery: Direction, Ethnicity and Mortality in the Transatlantic Slave Trade,* London, Frank Cass, 1997.

David Eltis and Stanley L. Engerman, *The Cambridge World History of Slavery: Volume 3 AD 1420 - AD 1804,* Cambridge, Cambridge University Press, 2011.

David Eltis, *Economic Growth and the Ending of the Transatlantic Slave Trade,* Oxford, Oxford University Press, 1987.

David Eltis, *Europeans and the Rise of African Slavery in the Americas,* Cambridge, Cambridge University Press, 2000.

David Northrup, *The Atlantic Slave Trade,* Lexington, D. C. Heath and Company, 1994.

Herbert S. Klein, *The Atlantic Slave Trade: Second Edition,* Cambridge, Cambridge University Press, 2005.

Holger Weiss, *Ports of Globalization, Places of Creolization: Nordic Possessions in the Atlantic World during the Era of the Slave Trade*, Boston, Brill, 2016.

J. Cañizares-Esguerra, M. D. Childs, and J. Sidbury, *The Black Urban Atlantic in the Age of the Slave Trade*, Philadelphia, University of Pennsylvania Press, 2013.

James A. Rawley and Stephen D. Behrendt, *The Transatlantic Slave Trade: A History*, Lincoln, University of Nebraska Press, 2005.

Jeremy Black, *The Atlantic Slave Trade in World History*, New York, Routledge, 2015.

John Thornton, *Africa and Africans in the Making of the Atlantic World - 1400-1680*, Cambridge, Cambridge University Press, 1992.

Leonardo Marques, *The United States and the Transatlantic Slave Trade to the Americas: 1776-1867*, New Haven, Yale University Press, 2016.

Philip D. Curtin, *The Atlantic Slave Trade - A Census*, Madison, University of Wisconsin Press, 1969.

Philip Misevich and Kristin Mann, *The Rise and Demise of Slavery and the Slave Trade in the Atlantic World*, Rochester, University of Rochester Press, 2016.

Rebecca Shumway, *The Fante and the Transatlantic Slave Trade*, Rochester, University of Rochester Press, 2011.

Robin Law, *The Slave Coast of West Africa 1550-1750*, Oxford, Oxford University Press, 1991.

Seymour Drescher, *From Slavery to Freedom: Comparative Studies in the Rise and Fall of Atlantic Slavery*, London, Macmillan Press LTD, 1999.

Srividhya Swaminathan, *Debating the Slave Trade: Rhetoric of British National Identity - 1759-1815*, Surrey, Ashgate Publishing, 2009.

Theodore M. Sylvester, *Slavery throughout the History - Almanac*, Detroit, UXL, 1999.

CPSIA information can be obtained
at www.ICGtesting.com
Printed in the USA
LVHW061959170722
723706LV00003B/39

9 781637 16205